FAITH OR REASON

REASON

CAN SCIENCE SILENCE GOD?

SAM OPUTA

outskirtspress

DENVER, COLORADO

Contents

Contents

Preface

I have read of many very intelligent people who proclaim decisively—and derisively—that there is no God. I have had a run-in with an astrophysicist, those who study the branch of astronomy that deals with the physics of stellar phenomena, who, after I inquired if he had doubts about the existence of intelligent beings, angrily and categorically declared, "I do not doubt. I am stating that there are *no* intelligent beings *anywhere*." It made me wonder why NASA is spending billions of dollars searching for life (any life) outside our planet. To this group, it has always been science and technology. I have also heard many highly educated folks say that they believe in God through faith. I do not hold any of these groups of people responsible for their beliefs or lack thereof. For me, atheism is not about a demolition of personal belief of theism, it is more a defense of reality and reason. It is only when a belief system maneuvers to claim itself as truth and force itself on others through indoctrination, or attempt to modify behaviors of others based on its tenets, or deny human rights, or actively inspire divisiveness, discrimination, and cause harm that reasoning people then have to act accordingly through reason and logic.

It would appear as though there is no real need to even identify as atheist as a political necessity were it not for the violations against humanity described above. To some, the concept of theism is perceived as inherently harmful to mankind, for history shows it has always been.

Is this brainwashing or brain washing?

For the faithful, it will always be shock and awe, dazzle and delight, and confusions galore, yet it remains in their mind—not just a book. It is Bible unquestioned. It does not matter whether anyone believes in something or nothing—- for that isn't any of my worries. People will advance reasons to do something or nothing. That is how the world goes. Just like crooks looking for suckers and suckers falling for crooks. Tops looking for bottoms as bottoms look for tops, in the same manner boys looking for girls and girls looking for boys. Whether anyone believes in any doctrine, as in this case, is as a result of misinformation or information accepted by "faith." There are too many confusing interpretations of the Bible. That there is a God is, without doubt, a truism for me. But you need to ask me *which God.* The mountain of evidence is there for the thinking mind to sift through and come to that understanding. The use of God here, though a singular, is a collective plurality of the Being(s) we call God.

There are a number of illogicalities in religious thinking. When you take your time to ponder over these illogicalities, you ask: Is the biblical God the correct model? You ask this because His take on love is questionable. From all the attributes and encomiums used to describe and praise Him, we can make some basic assumptions. We know, according to religious books, that:

> This/These God(s) created everything
> Evil is a subset of everything
> Therefore, God created evil.

Further, there can be no free will if this biblical God exists outside of time and at all times. What this absurdity means is that biblical God, existing in tomorrow, has already seen you and me live our lives and played our parts here on earth. Thus, there is nothing you and I could do that would prevent us from modifying our behaviors as He has already seen us behave—good or bad. Are you getting confused? Don't be confused; after all, this is what they have been teaching us. He knows my today and my tomorrow. If He does, how come religion turns its head upside to say biblical God has given man free will? This is as unchangeable as that which He saw me do yesterday, today, or even tomorrow. If this is the case, how can we have free will as a result? This isn't God anticipating what I will do today or tomorrow because He has seen all of my tomorrows. Remember the story of Abraham and Isaac and the test of faith if Isaac would be sacrificed by his father? If you put on your thinking cap, the outcome of this test of faith is twofold: One, kill Isaac, and two, not kill Isaac. That, you will think, is easy enough. Dice have six sides: one, two, three, four, five, and six. When a die is tossed, the chance of getting a seven is impossible because seven cannot be one of the outcomes. We know what the outcomes are likely to be though we do not know for certain, but we can predict it. We are guaranteed 16.67 percent certainty that the outcome is one of the six. We can get a one, two, three, four, five, or six. That God had to conduct this test of faith on Abraham where we know that the outcome could only be one of two shows that this God too does not claim to know everything. That some believers, however, want to acknowledge Him as all-knowing makes you wonder sometimes if God is a creation of man. If you did not know any better, you probably would think so too.

Let us look at this differently: If, as humans, and perchance, I could change what God, as all-knowing, has already observed me do, then I am overruling God as He will now be in error at that moment He saw me. For, even though I do not know my tomorrow, He knows my tomorrow, for He has seen me in tomorrow. In fact, following this logic through, then, even God can have no free will as He has already seen Himself do everything for He exists without time and in time. Are you confused? Brace yourself for you shall read of more confusing statements and doubts that fuel—or extinguish—beliefs not founded on reason but based on faith. This all boils down to a confusing web of nonsense and paradox— the belief without evidence, logic, and reason that religions pulls us into. Like I pointed out earlier, believers acknowledge that God is all-knowing, all-powerful, and all-loving. But there exists many problems in the world today. And there are quite a lot of serious problems. If God is all-knowing and allows all these problems, and He is all-loving and goes to war as the God of war, then, He is not all-powerful since He has no control over the problems that existed and continue to exist. Put differently, if He knows all these problems and He is all-powerful, then He is not all-loving since the problems continue to exist. He is all-knowing, yet He created a situation in the future where He had to go to war.

God(s), therefore, cannot be all-loving, all-powerful, and all-knowing. Consequently, though God exists, He cannot exist having all these powers attributed to Him by man. Though He exists, man has created a God different from the one in the Bible. It is therefore not surprising that man, having been created by the Gods, has an expectation based on imagination of a God man wants and created.

Let's go even further. If God is all powerful, all-knowing, and all-loving, then it must be reasonable and logical that when He (they) created man, He (they) did so knowing exactly what choices we would make throughout any human's lifetime. If God has an expectation that a soon-to-be created man would be a sinner through and through and He goes ahead to create such a man with the understanding that such a man is full of the intent to indulge in sin—whatever that is—then God is very suspect in the creation of hell—where He intends to punish His creation. And the alluded intention to send such men to hell is equally suspect. I am not joking here. This is serious. This writer does not believe in a place called hell. So, are the interpreters of the holy books messing things up? You bet. They do not know any better.

Our argument may be that we humans are created with free will and that we make our decisions. If this is so and God is all knowing, He knows what choices we are going to make; therefore, He did create us knowing He will be sending you and me (sinners) to hell. You see, before you existed, you did not know you would exist, and after existence, you will not know you existed. Therefore, would not existing be preferable to an eternity of pain, torture, and torment in hell? Is that confusing? No doubt.

For if God has created people with the knowledge of exactly what choices they are going to make today, and tomorrow, it suggests that all human choices and actions are predetermined, and so, nullify the concept of free will. Can you be any more confused? That is the purpose of this book, and if you are not decoding and deconstructing these doubts and confusions, you are not following the arguments. You will have to stop and start all over.

CHAPTER 1

Benefit of Doubt

The disciple Thomas reveals an important benefit about doubts. In John 20:25, Thomas was known to have had this attitude of doubt. The other disciples therefore said unto him, "We have seen the Lord." But he said unto them, "Unless I shall see in His hands the print of the nails, and put my finger into the print of the nails, and thrust my hand into His side, I will not believe."

After His crucifixion and resurrection, Jesus appeared alive to His disciples. However, one of the original 12 disciples, Thomas Didymus, was not present for this visitation (John 20:24). After he has been told by the other disciples of Jesus' resurrection and personal visit, Thomas had "doubt" and wanted proof/evidence of the risen Jesus Christ in order to believe. The story is told of how Jesus, knowing Thomas's human frailty resulted in weakened belief, accommodated Thomas. Jesus did not castigate Thomas, neither was He disappointed, but happily provided the proof. It is important to note that Jesus Christ did not have to yield to Thomas's request. But was it not the same Thomas who had volunteered to die with Jesus Christ? Many people have come to see Thomas as only a doubter, but the Bible never describes Thomas this way. Though the Bible describes his one moment of doubt, the Bible also described other moments of Thomas. His identity, despite our perception and description of him, is not rooted in only that one moment. There is much that is praiseworthy about him. This was demonstrated when Jesus, hearing of His friend Lazarus's sickness in Bethany, tells the disciples that they are returning there, and some of them protest: *people want to kill you there, Jesus*. But it was Thomas Didymus who spoke out: "Let us also go," he said, "that we may die with him" (John 11:8, 16). These are hardly the words of a proof-seeking doubter.

Thomas had spent 3 years intimately acquainted with Jesus, witnessing all His miracles and hearing His prophecies about His coming death and resurrection. The testimony Thomas received from the other 10 disciples about Jesus' resurrection and return to the disciples should have been enough, but yet he doubted.

What was he thinking? Now that epithet is stuck. Thomas is a doubter, The Doubter—the doubter's patron saint. His name comes conjoined, hip to bone, feather to wing, with that unshakable epithet: ***Doubting Thomas.***

Yet, Thomas's moment of doubt has comforted us so much for so long. It reflects to us our own ignorant and fragile beliefs, our own waywardness and wavering and yet tenacity—that our remembrance of that moment has, for most of us, eclipsed everything else about Thomas Didymus. It is a truth about Thomas that when dwelt upon obsessively, has become a myth about him, a character lapse that has become his all-defining character trait. That is Thomas's unflattering moment. Don't we all have our own unflattering moments, even though we keep them to ourselves? Is this entirely unfortunate? After all, Thomas's doubt itself is pithy and real. Thomas's is a doubt that often taunts us. It is a doubt that has traumatized the world's unbelieving, believing, and doubting. Many people today still harbor such doubts because the doubt is a reasonable one. His doubt is simply this: is Jesus really raised from the dead? His doubts perhaps got enhanced to: Has He really conquered death, or is the claim that He is raised just the deluded wishful desire of a few disciples whose desire for fulfillment of Jesus' teachings is uppermost in their religious priority? Is this a design by the other apostles who had been made unstable by grief, needing to fabricate a resurrection story to console them and to vindicate their "naïve" faith?

If you really think about it, is this not our doubt too? Thomas's doubt is our doubt. It is many Christians' nemesis and companion. It is a secret thought for all men who are gifted with the ability to free think. It is our secret haunting. The number of freethinkers who have this doubt is growing; after all, freethinkers are the ones to quickly allude to "unless I see it with my own eyes, touch it with my own hands, I will continue to question this belief." That has been the heart of the matter. That has been what stands between believing and doubting: unless I see and verify. Jesus Himself saw the logical air tightness and empiricism in Thomas's doubt and obliged Thomas's request to see it, touch it, and have the experience of it, to eliminate all shades of doubt. If then I, a freethinker, ask many questions, it is OK because I know it is just the right thing to do. As far as I am concerned, it is beginning to seem like it is easier to believe by faith than by reason. But, I refuse to do that. I will find the facts to help you, and I make a sound logical and informed decision based on facts.

There has never been a singularity of interpretation when it comes to the books "written" by God. We are aware of the differing views which many good holy books' readers hold about doctrines. It is a gathering heads of holy books for which must be believed unquestioned--hook, line, and sinker, for they are sticking to the story. There are groups of people that belong to the same umbrella of faith, but they interpret the same verses from their holy books differently. You may wonder why this is so. It is so because the holy books created confusion, and that confusion is manifest in the interpretations and practices of that faith. One instance is where Christians proclaim that no one had seen God and lived to tell about the encounter. Yet there are instances in the same Bible where people had seen God and lived. Indeed, there was a wrestling match between God and man, and God could not pin the man down. This is not being made up. Genesis Chapter 32:28 states, And he said, "Thy name shall be called no more Jacob, but Israel; for as a prince hast thou power with God and with men, and hast prevailed."

²⁹ And Jacob asked him, and said, "Tell me, I pray thee, thy name." And he said, "Why is it that thou dost ask after my name?" And he blessed him there.

³⁰ And Jacob called the name of the place Peniel [that is, The face of God]: "For I have seen God face to face, and my life is preserved."

It is all there in the Bible, and a careful read would reveal these to anyone. This is just one example. Another example is as affirmed in 1 Timothy 3:1.

In 1 Timothy 3:1–5 is a description of what the role of a bishop should be. We read, This is a true saying: If a man desire the office of bishop, he desireth a good work.

² A bishop then must be blameless, the husband of one wife, vigilant, sober, of good behavior, given to hospitality, apt at teaching;

³ not given to wine, not violent, not greedy for filthy lucre, but patient, not a brawler, not covetous;

⁴ one who ruleth well his own house, having his children in subjection with all dignity.

⁵ (For if a man know not how to rule his own house, how shall he take care of the church of God?)

What the above chapter and verses are making clear to all is that bishops and clergy can marry and do all things married folks do. However, in the real world, the doctrine has been turned over on its head and propagated as that where marriage is discouraged among the clergy of certain faiths. Some other faiths, meanwhile, do participate in the concept of marriage and harvest the fruits thereof. These are just two examples of doctrines gone wild in practice. That some people continue to say that there is no confusion in the Bible or that there is no confusion in the interpretation of the Bible again shows how some have been under the yoke of delusion. The confusion and disagreements are so sharp and varied, you need not look far to answer the question of why there are so many different denominations within Christianity. I choose Christianity here because 1. It is the most popular religion worldwide, and 2. I am a practitioner of Christianity. I can thus write about it based on the teachings I received without fear of accusation of being biased. Having said that, it is worth noting that confusion, misinterpretation, and different sects are not unique to Christianity. Islam—perhaps the second-most popular religion on earth, has the same issues worldwide too.

I suppose that there was never an intention for the church to be divided up into the hundreds of competing groups teaching vastly different doctrines. After all, Christians claim that their God—Yahweh—is not the God of confusion. In defense, they claim man is to blame for all the confusion. When are these people ever going to give man some respite? Everything that has gone wrong, they have blamed man. The Holy Book claims God always dealt harshly with man because man was nothing but evil. They suddenly forget to mention that this God is credited in the Bible with the creation of mankind—"evil" mankind. His first set of man He destroyed, thinking perhaps the descendants of Noah would suddenly become "not evil." Yep, that is a contradiction in the immutability presentation of a God they would also say is omnipresent.

Now man is blaming self again because of the many incontrovertible evidences that show that the Bible is full of confusion, repetitions, contradictions, and what have you. The confusions from the Holy Book are sometimes so deep that sects such as Jehovah's Witnesses and

Mormons could hardly be recognized as Christians that hold firmly to the creed of the Virgin birth and the Trinity. It is confusion galore, and no one is advocating here who is right or wrong. Around the world there are over 11 main religions and over 10,001 sects. Of these, some 6,000 exist in countries in regional Africa. Over 1,300 are in the United States, and thousands more scattered across the planet. If this is not confusion emanating from the interpretation of the Bible, I wonder what is. Again, this is not synonymous with the Bible believers. Other holy books have the same issues.

A lot of creationists have become equally so confused. They are so confused and shameless though they remain steadfast even as they know the doctrines they espouse are doomed. They hang on to the dogma that is consistently and stubbornly insistent that the Bible be taken and accepted as divine. At other times when apparent confusions are pointed out, they caution that the Bible must not be interpreted literally. They must be scoring a lot of soccer goal points with the continual shifts of the goal posts. They say that:

1. The earth was created in 6 days,

2. The earth is only 6,000 years old, and they also say

3. That man did not evolve.

On #1, when science came up with explanation on the universe's age of 13.7 billion years, the creationists' 6 days of creation suddenly had a new meaning. (Read *Why Was Man Created?*)

That some people still estimate earth's existence at 6,000 years is mind-boggling. That, in itself, is an elephant of confusion. As science continues to evolve with new findings, it will be difficult for creationists' views to stand the test of time. In fact, most of their views are almost out of vogue/style/contention so much so that they are withering in the face of scientific findings and development, and, although they may not be facing complete extinction, ultimate obscurity is its destination.

When it becomes absolutely impossible to logically explain any given event, the Bible-thumpers resort to these various methods listed below, in no order of importance, to explain away illogical texts. Very often they say:

1. "God works in mysterious ways." This is another of the "that is a miracle" excuse. This is a useful tool to dodge interpreting the unknown or misunderstood. A useful tool for when the speaker does not understand the conflict between what the Bible texts are and what the interpreter wishes they were.

2. "There is more to this than meets the eye." This is used when one verse (A) says something, and another verse (B) says something contradicting to verse (A). These are often the same Bible-thumping people that insist theirs is the only possible interpretation.

3. "That is to be taken metaphorically." In other words, what is written is not what is meant. I find this comical and entertaining. Who are those who decide what is or is not to be taken as the absolute Word of God? This dumb excuse is an excuse to misinterpret the books to suit their intended doctrines.

4. "Must be interpreted and understood in context." This method is age-old, and it is perhaps the best tool for deception. You must have observed preachers flipping through the Bible pages, quoting a verse here and there from various books, hardly reading any complete story with all the accompanying events. They pick and choose these verses to weave the story they want to tell. As an exercise, think of any story you would like to tell, and there are verses you could pull from the books to match your story, even when those texts have nothing in context to your story. I find this quite amusing because it reminds me of magicians who, when they are performing, make you recognize

that the more you look, the less you understand. This technique is well employed by preachers. Whether preachers do this with intent to psychologically attune your thinking or they do this in ignorance is unknown to me. But if I must place a bet, I would place that bet on the side of ignorance. I find this very interesting because it comes from the same crowd whose modus operandi is to push extracted verses that support a given view. However, the Catholic church does not do this. They present complete stories as first and second readings.

5. "That was a common simple copying or writing error." The intent of this is to place the error on the writer not the speaker. It is as if the writer had hearing problems, and the speaker's intent is different from the texts. This is transcription error, like in accounting where a number like 79 was written as 97. Thus, an incorrect number was copied instead of the right one. In other words, what was quoted was not really what was really said. It is not the writer's (prophet) fault but just what the author thought was said. This is an apparent admission that the Bible is not divine after all, for, oops, there is a mistake. This work is simply about mistakes and confusions—I will take it anyway it comes. No defense explanations needed.

6. "That is a miracle." Obviously, this is a euphemism for "what we cannot logically explain is naturally a miracle." Suddenly, miracles are accepted as facts.

Even if one is not an avid reader of the Holy Book, one can decipher the God presented in the Old Testament as a God of war and a God who engineered and participated in mass killings contrasted with the God presented by Jesus in the New Testament—a God of peace and love. If this is not misrepresentation, contradiction, and confusion from the Holy Book, I wonder what is.

When Christians speak about Yahweh, they present Him as a God that unfathomably loves and whose wrath reflects His perfect justice. Perfect justice? What is perfect in such crude execution of misguided rules? Christians and some others narrate a tale in which He is utterly sovereign, yet He personally interacts with other deities, the least—the human beings He "made" in His own image, such that He holds them accountable for what they say and do and feel and imagine; for sovereign though He is, He never treats them as creations with free will. God, they claim, is one, yet they also claim He exists as three persons who interact with one another. Even to begin to make sense of these complementary truths, it would not be long before one is wrestling with the relationships within and between the makeup of the Trinity.

A doctrine that cannot stand up to examination is one not worthy of being accepted. This does not mean that we can hold God and put Him in a tube in a laboratory to make tests for verification. The examination through evidence in narration texts are already there for us to grasp and examine. For example, the major holy books contradict one another on matters of Trinity even while acknowledging all the biblical prophets, Mary, and Jesus. When you do some critical analysis, you will arrive at a conclusion that most denominations are mixtures of varying degrees of spiritual dogmas, spiritual error, and truths, and are basically the doctrines of men. It is, therefore, best to celebrate the things that are right, true, and self-evident that also point to and expose those things that are illogically conceived. To do otherwise will be harmful to what we concluded to celebrate in the first place. If it is wrong, no amount of artful dodging rationalizations can make it right.

Some would shout holy mackerel! here but read, understand, and interpret the Bible on your own. It is not a secret that God killed with reckless abandon and sought praises for such dastardly acts. That Christians use these killings as a praiseworthy theme of a war God protecting a group from enemies is even more confusing portrayed as in its interpretation. If there was one God, how can that one God kill its creation to save its creation? Is there no better way? It's even more confusing to make a choice to serve a God who has, from the early beginning, chosen Israel as His people. Some apologists will, of course, come up with various excuses to defend the God of the Old Testament, but such arguments are simply illogical.

This work, therefore, is to show the many contradictions, confusion, and misrepresentations found in the Holy Book—the Bible. Do not forget to always bear in mind as you read this work, that the Bible has been proclaimed a book inspired by divine guidance.

If your awareness level is low and your thinking is mired in shame and guilt resulting from years of religious indoctrination, you can be excused for subscribing to a set of doctrines that can help you move to what you believe is a "higher" level of awareness. However, your mind-set will remain incredibly dysfunctional as you are merely swapping one form of erroneous thinking for another.

For reasonably logical-thinking persons, religion is a ridiculously consciousness-lowering doctrine. It has been and will ever be. Sometimes, I just wonder why we are told that we cannot do good deeds if not by the grace of the doctrines taught to us. It is as if we were built to do evil and evil only. That whenever you do something good, it is by the grace of some being(s). While it is worthy to mention that some tested beliefs can be empowering, on the whole, the decision to formally participate in a faith-based religion will ultimately burden your mind with a gargantuan load of false notions.

I have been quizzed on the subject of individual choices otherwise known as free will. I have had to explain that the decision of an individual to follow a set of doctrines is that person's free will. It is simple. When your doctrines include principles which say, "Do this or you die," you become a prisoner to such concepts. You cannot give free will with the right hand and give me rules and regulations with the other. That is simply no free will.

When you subscribe to a religion and its attendant doctrines, you have substituted nebulous group-think for precise, independent thoughts. Instead of learning to discern truth on your own, you're told what to believe. Instead of learning the formulated truth, you are fed the "truth" of a group whose intentions are seriously questionable. This, rather than accentuate your learning and thinking abilities, confines what you must learn and think. This route will never accelerate your spiritual growth; instead, it clips the wings of the helicopter, as it were, on your conscious process for flying into the realms of learning and development. Though I numbered below these dos and don'ts, they are in no particular order of importance. Logical-thinking people would not borrow from religion the following concepts or acts. They just know it's either right or wrong.

1.   You cannot kill a fellow human

2.   You cannot take another person's stuff

3.   You cannot talk ill of a person who can squeeze the waste product out of you in their face

4.   You cannot park your car in a no parking zone for the penalty is some money out of your pockets

5.   You can help a hungry man with some food

6.   Stop and help a vehicular accident victim on a highway

7.   Call the police when your neighbor is under a threat of bodily harm

8.   Inform the authorities when you know society is in imminent danger

If the Holy Book crunchers are truly conversant with their books, they will find where God Himself knew and was elated that man would use his intellect. That observation by God was recorded in Genesis 11:6. Read that verse a few times and it will register. Man's intellect is a far better instrument of spiritual growth than many doctrines taught to you at a given location daily with hopes that such teachings would save you from the doctrine of hell.

We definitely would not begrudge an individual for choosing some put-together doctrines celebrated as religions. To do so is to deny a perceived "free will." The best line of action is to put together an intelligent, yet simple and full of commonsense arguments to make that individual see reason and make a personal ultimate call. I will, however, not want to come across as the man in the story below.

An incident that remains indelible in my mind to this very day is this story. A man went to dip in a river on a very hot day of over 107 degrees Fahrenheit (42 degrees Celsius). After taking off his clothes, he jumped in. While enjoying the freshness and coolness of the water, a naked crazy man came lurking around. Suddenly the crazy man grabbed the clothes of the man in the water and ran. The man rushed out of the water and gave chase. As they ran through the grassy walk path on the bank of the river, other observers looked on in amazement as two adult males ran, one chasing the other. They were not attracted by the nakedness of either men who, by this time, ran into the streets of the town. They were wondering, when did the man in the river go insane too? As far as the onlookers were concerned, they were witnessing *two* crazy people running naked.

Before assessment of what the man in the water could have done rightly or wrongly, let us look at the conflict and the confusion created among the two naked participants and the onlookers in the above story.

There are people who have been so religiously indoctrinated that they would kill to defend the doctrine. They are insane. And there are those who call themselves moderates with their chest deep in the mud of indoctrination and neck high in free will. The moderates would defend themselves by claiming they are sane since they do not kill in defense of the doctrine. Who are they fooling? Themselves!

Most people are born into the religion they practice. They knew that religion since they were babies. They became adults in that religion. They are yet to delve into and critically ask questions to seek some answers to the many contrasts and confusions inherent in the religion they have practiced since birth. Being born into a religion does not make that religion the best avenue to save oneself from the created doctrine of hell. If you read the book *God Is Not Enough, Messiah Needed*, you would read or learn from my opinions on whether or not hell is real. It is really, really pathetic how we believe that, hook, line, and sinker. I say so because I was once in that ship powered and ruddered by the winds to a destination called *Nowhere*.

If there are five babies born in each continent, the likelihood that the one born in United States, Europe, and South America would be a Christian is high. In Africa, the chance of being a Christian or Muslim is 50/50, and in the Middle East, a 100 percent chance being Muslim can be assumed.

Meanwhile, there is a chance that a child born in the USA and other Western countries would grow to become an atheist. The chances that an African adult would grow into an animist while pretending to be affiliated with the most popular doctrines are also very high. (The above statistical data is an assumption.) Some will never outgrow their baby religions. But what if these five babies' locations/cultures were swapped? The probability that the outcomes in religion of each baby would change is 100 percent; however, the chance that location/culture/upbringing will change is less than 5 percent.

What the above statistical example is driving at is that our belief systems are just a product of your environment/culture/upbringing and not a conscious choice of a given individual.

Doctrines, no matter how and where you get them, are just like a salad. It is a mishmash of vegetables and dairy products. Any one chef can make a variety of salads from those products. There are so many religions with various doctrines that you start to wonder if these religions are from the same chef/god. If these doctrines are from same source, that source must be wanting in manipulation and dissemination of information.

Are you still practicing the religion you happened to be born into, believing it hook, line, and sinker? Surely you've outgrown your baby clothes by now. Isn't it time you also outgrew your baby religion?

What if you were born into a different culture? Would you have been conscious enough to find your way back to your current belief system? Or are your current beliefs merely a product of your environment and not the result of conscious choice?

At this point, I am tempted to go into a minimal narration of religious history, but then, that is not the intention of this book.

Some years ago, one of my pastors preached on how no one has ever seen God and how God cannot be seen. That was, and still is, a lie, by the way. Read evidence found in: Genesis 17:1, 18:1, 26:2, 32:30; Exodus 24:9–11, and the whopper of them all, Exodus 33:11. "And the Lord spoke unto Moses face to face, as a man speaketh unto his friend. And he returned again into the camp; but his servant Joshua, the son of Nun, a young man, departed not out of the tabernacle."

However, to give my pastor the benefit of the doubt, he might have been using the narration of the burning bush where Yahweh first had an encounter with Moses, or he might have been using Exodus 33:20. And He said, "Thou canst not see My face, for there shall no man see Me and live."

Either way you look at it, you have just been introduced to the contrasts, contradictions, and misinterpretations in one of the books used to introduce religious doctrines. This is the main cheese on the cracker— the plump meat on the bone of the matter.

As my pastor preached, he would pause momentarily for an applause and the common yells of halleluiahs and amens. I just listened and waited for the sermon to be over. It was like one of those sermons where I listened and went home to study the book to corroborate the sermons. Most often, I found out that the pastors were misinterpreting the words in the Bible or that they did not read the contrasting and confusing verses to understand the words before disseminating the same. As if these were not bad enough, there was the outright substitution of generally accepted practices in an effort to introduce new doctrines. If that church was a Catholic one, I would have assumed that the pastor was merely following laid-down interpretation from Rome. But it was not. My pastor was as uninformed, and perhaps more dangerous, than some layperson who never read the Bible. It was pathetic, and here he was, leading many people to a place called *Nowhere*.

I am not telling you or advocating that there is no God. I am not subscribing to some notions out there that there is no Jesus Christ. I am, however, talking about doctrines and how these doctrines came to be. Did Jesus lay down any doctrine? What I remember is that He sowed love, the love that is of two kinds: the love for God and a love for your fellow man. That is all. That is how I surmised what I read. But then, is that a doctrine or commonsense free will? All other insinuation is an attempt at making doctrines malleable to suit whoever is making a case for creation of yet another doctrine. Meanwhile, the love of God and for which God is yet another question.

Now, do I have any antagonizing, disrespectful, look-down or bring-down syndrome toward my pastors? Of course not. I understand that my pastors and many others before them are all victims of brainwashing that has gone on for eons of years. Even the occupants of the highest offices in religions engage in this doctrine propaganda. They too are brainwashed through indoctrination. They are no better than slaves serving the master's command. They are enforcing and/or creating more doctrines many years after the death of Jesus Christ. And they truly and faithfully believe they are carrying out a mandate.

CHAPTER 2

The All-Loving, All-Powerful Part

THE ALL-LOVING PART:

What is love, after all? We need to explain love so that we can evaluate if God is capable of love, or if man invented the love attribute for God. No matter how we define it, love is a biological feeling. I must emphasis the word "biological" here. If it is biological, can God feel love since He is not biological but divine? How would anyone know this, to even associate such attributes to an all-loving, all-powerful, almighty biblical God? Biologically, love is a neurological condition just like the feeling of hunger or thirst. And just like hunger and thirst would occur and reoccur many times a day over a period of one's life, love, however, is more permanent over a period of time. Sometimes, it's a lifetime. We talk about love being blind or unconditional, in the sense that we have no control over it. But then, that is not so surprising since love is basically chemistry.

Let us look at love and its meaning in detail. The one answer to detail *love* remains elusive in part because love is not one thing. There is the love we have for our parents. Love for our children. Love for country. And even love for God(s). It is important to note, however, that love has different qualities and variants. Love can be conditional and unconditional, steadfast or fickle. At its best, all variants of love are a kind a passionate commitment that people develop and nurture. Love, when not nurtured and without commitment, becomes a mere infatuation. Infatuation fades over time. Considering the above explanations of love, I am not satisfied yet about the true meaning of love, for nothing expresses love better than the bond between a mother and child or father and child. I introduced the love of parents for children because it is unconditional. This love is so biological; a mother becomes fearless when confronted with a dangerous situation to save her child, even if she pays with her life. Fathers do that too. That is the ultimate love.

Now that we have been led to believe through the creation of man that God loves us so much that He let His only begotten son to die for our sins, it would be necessary to examine this type of love. But first, let us get that information from the Bible.

THE ALL-POWERFUL PART:

Love and power do not coalesce. It is very difficult for any entity wielding power to truly show love in all its variations. It is equally almost impossible for the entity filled with love to exercise power in such a way that it would not infringe on love. The entities that have come closest to exercising both power and love best at any given time are parents. Even at that, there are a few parents who just cannot exercise power and love. If you seriously investigate the behaviors and learn from those who profess to exercise power and love, it takes minutes to extrapolate that love is distinct just as power is. It is difficult using both as tools at the same time for good, simultaneously, over a long period of time. Those that can do such are few, and they include mothers, fathers, sons, and daughters. The aforementioned if in power could use such power to save a son from execution because of love. But, love without power cannot save "self."

Many people talk about love for country. Some profess love until they are in and wielding power. In exercise of power, some leaders will go to war. Is the war an act of love? Maybe love for country, but people will die in the war. Wouldn't love of mankind tamper the power of a leader? Are you beginning to see the conflict of love and power? Let us go a little further and take it to the ultimate circumstance.

Let us see how all-powerful trumps all-loving. Read for yourself and be cognizant of who gave the order.

Numbers 31:6–18

[6] And Moses sent them to the war, a thousand of every tribe, them and Phinehas the son of Eleazar the priest, to the war, with the holy instruments, and the trumpets to blow in his hand.

[7] And they warred against the Midianites, as the Lord commanded Moses; and they slew all the males.

[8] And they slew the kings of Midian, beside the rest of them that were slain; namely, Evi, and Rekem, and Zur, and Hur, and Reba, five kings of Midian: Balaam also the son of Beor they slew with the sword.

[9] And the children of Israel took all the women of Midian captives, and their little ones, and took the spoil of all their cattle, and all their flocks, and all their goods.

[10] And they burnt all their cities wherein they dwelt, and all their goodly castles, with fire.

[11] And they took all the spoil, and all the prey, both of men and of beasts.

[12] And they brought the captives, and the prey, and the spoil, unto Moses, and Eleazar the priest, and unto the congregation of the children of Israel, unto the camp at the plains of Moab, which are by Jordan near Jericho.

[13] And Moses, and Eleazar the priest, and all the princes of the congregation, went forth to meet them without the camp.

¹⁴ And Moses was wroth with the officers of the host, with the captains over thousands, and captains over hundreds, which came from the battle.

¹⁵ And Moses said unto them, Have ye saved all the women alive?

¹⁶ Behold, these caused the children of Israel, through the counsel of Balaam, to commit trespass against the Lord in the matter of Peor, and there was a plague among the congregation of the Lord.

¹⁷ Now therefore kill every male among the little ones, and kill every woman that hath known man by lying with him.

¹⁸ But all the women children, that have not known a man by lying with him, keep alive for yourselves.

Some would argue that the love of Israel is the reason Yahweh went out all charged to protect His beloved people. But then, where is the love for the killed and vanquished here? Remember, the attributes in question here are ALL-LOVING & ALL-POWERFUL.

Exodus 15:3: The Lord is a man of war: the Lord is his name.

All Exodus 15:3 is explaining here is that this God—Yahweh—is a God of war as opposed to all-loving. Love for the Jews? I hear you reason. Are not those killed in war God's children too? Whether He created all mankind or not is not the issue at discussion here. It is the all-powerful and all-loving attributes of this biblical God.

And from Genesis 6, it was concluded to destroy man. Where is the all-loving? I see all-powerful. Let us read some parts of Genesis 6, King James Version (KJV):

6 And it came to pass, when men began to multiply on the face of the earth, and daughters were born unto them,

[2] That the sons of God saw the daughters of men that they were fair; and they took them wives of all which they chose.

[3] And the Lord said, My spirit shall not always strive with man, for that he also is flesh: yet his days shall be an hundred and twenty years.

[4] There were giants in the earth in those days; and also after that, when the sons of God came in unto the daughters of men, and they bare children to them, the same became mighty men which were of old, men of renown.

[5] And God saw that the wickedness of man was great in the earth, and that every imagination of the thoughts of his heart was only evil continually.

[6] And it repented the Lord that he had made man on the earth, and it grieved him at his heart.

[7] *And the Lord said, I will destroy man whom I have created from the face of the earth; both man, and beast, and the creeping thing, and the fowls of the air; for it repenteth me that I have made them.*

Then, for you and I, have you considered heaven or earth? I guess some probably have. I, for one, have no evidence of hell. I have no evidence because hell was not created. Stop the doubt and read the book of creation and see for yourself that hell was not mentioned because it was not created. For those who manufactured hell, it is akin to shifting the goal posts during a football match. And yes, what else was manufactured? Purgatory. So laughable.

CHAPTER 3

Hell Contradicts Love

HELL has been described as a place for punishing the unrepentant sinners. From Adam to those who were on earth at the time of the great Flood, have you ever wondered if all the victims would ever inherit heaven? In one of my previous writings in the book *God Is Not Enough, Messiah Needed,* I had concluded that there is no such place as hell. But for those who would have been indoctrinated to believing that there is a hell, through faith, have you wondered to ask, "Would one be held in hell indefinitely for a definite number of years one was on earth committing sins?"

How can a justice system supposedly divine inflict such unending punishment for finite years of atrocities on earth? Is there compassion in that? Is there any sign of an all-loving attribute in that? I see an all-powerful trait in it, but nothing of love; thus, less of an all-loving trait.

We must come to an understanding that whoever is exercising the most power in a relationship is also exercising the least love, and whoever is expressing the most love has the least power and thus exercises the least power. It is so because a person must give up power to express love. This is because love makes an entity vulnerable. As we reason these things, you may find it difficult to comprehend if you have no clue of the reason why man was created.

You think you are the first to have doubts about the Holy Book? You think you are the first to question religion? You think that suddenly you are questioning your faith? Obviously, you are not the first, and you will not be the last. There are many who have questioned their faith. Some are so indoctrinated to question what they were taught. In my various discussions, theists typically end with "I choose to believe this," as though truth were a choice. It's not. What they just expressed there is "Faith." Some cling to the mantra "Faith starts where science ends." They fail to see this mantra as "Where knowledge ends, religion is introduced." Knowledge is ever conquering new frontiers and what some consider as faith today would become knowledge tomorrow.

Confusion! Confusion. They will tell others to believe, and when in doubt invoke faith. There are those who say faith starts where science ends. Would you believe that? This, as you know, creates more doubts. We are to believe by faith when the Gospels were written. These generations are inquisitive and enlightened and learned. We are no easy pushovers anymore. We will be doubly hardly harder to push over 1,000 years from now. What exactly is faith? Faith is when you believe in a supernatural entity without recourse to reason. Now, how did you know that there is a supernatural deity? You know because you were told. You knew because you were indoctrinated into accepting that what you were told perhaps when you were a child is true. Did you, at any point of your existence, sit yourself down and think for at least a moment about this, your supernatural deity? Do you know it is easier to believe by faith because to reason and gather the evidence to support your beliefs is much harder?

Personally, I do not believe by faith. I do not like that word—it is deceptive and makes one lazy. I know that Yahweh was here on earth. I also know that alias "Satan" was here on earth. I know also that their subordinates are being sent to earth on occasion. One of those occasions was also documented in Luke 1:26–35. There are many other occasions which were misinterpreted to mean things that were not intended.

Luke 1:26–35, King James Version (KJV):

26 And in the sixth month the angel Gabriel was sent from God unto a city of Galilee, named Nazareth,

27 To a virgin espoused to a man whose name was Joseph, of the house of David; and the virgin's name was Mary.

28 And the angel came in unto her, and said, Hail, thou that art highly favoured, the Lord is with thee: blessed art thou among women.

29 And when she saw him, she was troubled at his saying, and cast in her mind what manner of salutation this should be.

30 And the angel said unto her, Fear not, Mary: for thou hast found favour with God.

[31] And, behold, thou shalt conceive in thy womb, and bring forth a son, and shalt call his name Jesus.

[32] He shall be great, and shall be called the Son of the Highest: and the Lord God shall give unto him the throne of his father David:

[33] And he shall reign over the house of Jacob for ever; and of his kingdom there shall be no end.

[34] Then said Mary unto the angel, How shall this be, seeing I know not a man?

[35] And the angel answered and said unto her, The Holy Ghost shall come upon thee, and the power of the Highest shall overshadow thee: therefore also that holy thing which shall be born of thee shall be called the Son of God.

The subordinate referenced delivering this message above is a worker for his boss—God. Whether you call such workers angels, spirits, watchers, or extraterrestrials does not make a difference. What it confirms is that there are beings that were in existence prior to the creation of earth and man.

Now, do I believe the above by faith? Of course not. I believe it by evidence. And, yes, the evidence is abundant. In one of the areas in the Bible where faith was discussed, it indicates that faith is based on reason. Hebrews 11:1 defines **faith** as ". . . *the assurance of things hoped for, the conviction of things not seen.*"

Hebrews 11:1–11, King James Version (KJV):

11 Now faith is the substance of things hoped for, the evidence of things not seen.

[2] For by it the elders obtained a good report.

[3] Through faith we understand that the worlds were framed by the word of God, so that things which are seen were not made of things which do appear.

[4] By faith Abel offered unto God a more excellent sacrifice than Cain, by which he obtained witness that he was righteous, God testifying of his gifts: and by it he being dead yet speaketh.

[5] By faith Enoch was translated that he should not see death; and was not found, because God had translated him: for before his translation he had this testimony, that he pleased God.

[6] But without faith it is impossible to please him: for he that cometh to God must believe that he is, and that he is a rewarder of them that diligently seek him.

[7] By faith Noah, being warned of God of things not seen as yet, moved with fear, prepared an ark to the saving of his house; by the which he condemned the world, and became heir of the righteousness which is by faith.

[8] By faith Abraham, when he was called to go out into a place which he should after receive for an inheritance, obeyed; and he went out, not knowing whither he went.

[9] By faith he sojourned in the land of promise, as in a strange country, dwelling in tabernacles with Isaac and Jacob, the heirs with him of the same promise:

[10] For he looked for a city which hath foundations, whose builder and maker is God.

[11] Through faith also Sara herself received strength to conceive seed, and was delivered of a child when she was past age, because she judged him faithful who had promised.

I believe everything and more written above, not by faith . . . but by reason of evidence. Evidence abounds all over the place that the narratives above happened at a point in time.

For an individual to be rest assured and be convinced of anything or something, there needs to be evidence—that is the *ground for belief and proof—the evidence sufficient enough to establish some things as true, or to produce belief in its truth.*

This, however, does not work for everyone because not everyone is willing or capable of putting in the needed time to sit and read to understand all the evidence that is in the numerous subjects and "holy books" out there. You can, all by yourself, reduce the confusion by eliminating all the misinterpretations that have caused your questions to seem unanswerable. Most of your questions are answerable, especially if you start on the premise of "Why was man created?" I have helped with that question in the book *Why Was Man Created?*

LOVE/COMPASSION CONFUSION

Religious doctrines invariably hamper the development of conscience. It causes confusion. It causes serious troubles when misinterpreted. It is the source of some of the hatred of all sorts among man. Problems like pointless violence and warfare emanating from *my God is better than yours.* Is it not ironic that the major religions proclaiming the One God doctrine are the ones at each other's throat protecting their God? They all preach nonviolence as a doctrine, yet at the slightest provocation, they become the most violent of all. Historically, violence has ever been the path for sons and daughters of any particular religion. Religions, generally, were at one point or another married to violence. Whether justified or not, religions today still engage in violence. Whether implemented by followers or implemented by governments does not really matter. Some may casually think this is a small matter. It is not. Can you imagine a nuclear weapon in the hands of some religious fanatics? I shudder at the thought of that. They will just annihilate nonbelievers in their faith in a twinkle of an eye, and the sad part is that they will believe they are carrying out God's mandate.

Nuclear weapons are definitely safer in the hands of freethinkers. Religious apologists cannot be trusted as they will quickly (based on past behaviors) violate a value a freethinker holds to be true at all times.

If one is to love based on some doctrines, what would happen if those doctrines are no longer held to be true? When love becomes a set of doctrines, it is external; therefore, it is not the kind of love of a free will. It is no longer a conscious choice type of love. It becomes a free will forced down the throat through doctrines. This is like a hard, large, square pill to swallow. The religious apologists aka religious fanatics are the least loving of peoples populating this earth. This is why. The more indoctrinated a person becomes, the less compassionate they become. Though they have the illusion of compassion, they cannot see through their bigotry, because their compassion is like a mirage.

An indoctrinated individual will not let another from another kind of indoctrination to marry his/her daughter, sister, brother, etc. Some would not eat at the same table with you because you are of a different "God," even when they all profess the One God. If those who profess God have no chance at a table, I wonder what nonbelievers' chances would be.

Their sense of hate is nonexistent because they know not that bigotry is hate. Nothing is as gross as hating while not knowing you hate. Such persons are very dangerous to self and to mankind. They are not accepting of anyone and everyone who has not been indoctrinated as they have. They erroneously believe they are better than you and that those not indoctrinated in their beliefs are the scum of the earth. They believe they are collaborators with some higher "being" to help galvanize the scum of human beings into unconscious slavery to that "being," even though they themselves know little or nothing of it.

They believe they are acting in compassion. But they hardly can fathom that unconditional love can only result from conscious choice—the free will to choose without the threat of punishment or the promise of reward. I am not advocating the abandonment of doctrines through religions, but we must stop giving a face, hands, and legs that do not belong to religion. We are lucky to have Founding Fathers that long time ago saw the need for a concept known as the separation of church and state. Even so, we are still in a garbage heap of confusion.

CHAPTER 4

Introducing a Few Good Contradictions

The various religions on the planet acknowledge and thus attest by their actions, voluntarily or otherwise, the contradictions, contrasts, misinterpretations, disagreements, and what have you about God's words or statutes in the many stories of the good book. Do your own study and write down all the observable differences you can notice among readers of the books of the Bible and you may wonder why it is so. If they didn't, how do we explain the existence of thousands of religions all claiming to come from one source? Even with the Bible, there has been a mass production of various sects (Catholic and Protestants). And even among the Protestants, you have more protesting. Protestants!—That word! I love that word for in this matter you may want to ask—What are they protesting? They are protesting the confusion and "misrepresentation" and misinterpretation of the words of the Bible.

Some are so quick to say that there is no confusion, no contrasts, no misinterpretation, but this is funny because they are living the confusion day in and day out.

Some are quick to defend the book quoting unrelated verses from the body of chapters to prove why God does not create confusion whereas God Himself was in black and white as saying, let us go down and create confusion in man's one language. The only concluding logic one can draw from any verse or verses to contradict what God said in the book of Genesis about creating confusion for man is in itself a contradictory verse of the Bible; therefore, they confirm unwittingly the line of argument that there was and still is contradictions, contrasts, and misrepresentations in the Bible.

The Bible in its crudest form is more straightforward and honest than all the apologists, fanatics, and clergy that claim to live by its teachings. The Bible in all its honest narratives presented a God in His crude wickedness; a being lacking in tolerance, a warmonger, magician, a protector, and a God who sometimes is indecisive just like man whom He allegedly claims to have created. The Bible is so honest that sometimes it forgets it has an agenda—the agenda of those who chose the books that made up the Bible. To that extent, the Bible describes an event rather than expresses an opinion. It is therefore an event left to your interpretation. Hence, the many misinterpretations given to literal words by some clergy which are just that—literal.

Most often, you see the manipulation of the hand of man in the interpretations of the Bible, but try as they could, the truth of each chapter still shines through for those who have no set agenda. The Bible is simply a bank for knowledge to understanding beings who had been here eons of years before they decided to reengineer mankind to take their place on earth. If you understand these, you will ultimately come to a conclusion that all the maiming, killing, alienation, suffering, and all the wars that were fought just to promote monotheism and monotheistic teachings seem to have been a waste of effort and in itself, a war fought by confused minds. A war mandated by people whose minds were controlled by lunacy and confusion. For even after those wars were fought in the name of religion, the only legacy it left is not one of clear-cut monotheism. If there is anything clear-cut of a legacy, it is that of confusion. It is a legacy of confused monotheism. And as if all that isn't confusing enough, today, more than ever before, we have these supposedly definitive monotheist religions full of splinter groups, sects, factions, cliques, schisms, and in-fighting. When it comes to the attributes of God and the best way of worshipping Him, none of these sects and factions can agree on anything—and you can count yourself lucky if the discussion of religious matters does not terminate in explosions. There are so many different views of the One true God, it sometimes seems that all those schisms, factions, and sects are really desperately yearning for the good old days of polytheism, which is probably the ultimate irony.

The Bible is riddled with repetitions and contradictions, things that the Bible-bangers would be quick to point out in anything that they want to criticize. That there are illogicalities is not an overstatement. Even when there is logic, interpreters interpret in such a way to render such logic illogical. For instance, Genesis 1 and 2 disagree about the order in which things were created and how satisfied God is about the results of His labors. The Flood story is really two interwoven stories that contradict each other on how many of each kind of animal are to be brought into the ark—is it one pair each or seven pairs each of the "clean" ones? Going further, the Gospel of John disagrees with the other three Gospels on the activities of Jesus Christ (how long had He stayed in Jerusalem—a couple of days or a whole year?), and all four Gospels contradict each other on the details of Jesus Christ's last moments and resurrection. The Gospels of Matthew and Luke contradict each other on the genealogy of Jesus Christ's father, though both agree that Joseph was not his real father. Repetitions and contradictions are understandable for a hodgepodge collection of documents, but not for some carefully constructed treatise reflecting a well thought out plan.

Of the various methods I've seen to "explain" these are:

1. "That is to be taken metaphorically." In other words, what is written is not what is meant. I find this entertaining, especially for those who decide what isn't to be taken as other than the absolute Word of God—which just happens to agree with the particular thing they happen to want.

2. "There was more there than . . ." This is used when one verse says "there was an H," and another says, "there was a Y," so they decide there was an "H and a Y"—which is said nowhere. This makes them happy, since it does not say there was not "H and Y." This is often the same crowd that insists theirs is the only possible interpretation, meaning only "H" and that is the only way. I find it entertaining and hilarious when they do not mind adding to verses in question.

3. "It has to be understood in context." I find this amusing because it comes from the same crowd that likes to push extracted verses that support their particular view. Often it is just one of the verses in the contradictory set which is supposed to be taken as the truth when, if you add more to it, it suddenly becomes "out of context."

4. "There was just a copying/writing error." This is sometimes called a "transcription error," as in where one number was meant and an incorrect one was copied down. Or what was "quoted" wasn't really what was said, but just what the author thought was said. And that's right—I'm not disagreeing with events, I'm disagreeing with what is written. It would be easier to just admit that a mistake or misinterpretation just occurred.

5. "That is a miracle." Naturally. That is why it is stated as fact. What they fail to understand is easily dubbed a miracle.

6. "God works in mysterious ways." A useful dodge when the speaker doesn't understand the conflict between what the Bible implied and what they interpret it to mean.

CHAPTER 5

What Books Made the Bible?

Men, mostly the ones that have some interest in the protection of status quo, put these books together. They are what they are—men like you and me. They are no better or more divine than you and I. Truth be said, you and I are better educated than the men who put these books together. Given another circumstance and different men, you and I would be reading a different set of books. I just want you to bear that little info in mind as we go on.

The Bible is a canonical collection of texts considered sacred in Judaism as well as in Christianity. The term "Bible" is shared between the two religions, although the contents of each of their collections of canonical texts are not the same. Different religious groups include different books within their canons, in different orders, and sometimes divide or combine books or incorporate additional material into canonical books. If you start wondering why there are differences, you are not alone for therein lies the confusions that cause doubts within the religions and/or sects. However, the bigger question is: "Who were the authors of the books of the Bible?" Most believers will not hesitate to provide an answer. And the answer is— God. Ultimately, above the human authors, the Bible was written by God. Second Timothy 3:16 tells us that the Bible was "breathed out" by God. God superintended the human authors of the Bible so that, while using their own writing styles and personalities, they still recorded exactly what

God intended. It is, therefore, understood by all that follow the Word, that God is the real author behind all the books of the Bible. God, Himself, wrote, in stone, the Ten Commandments for Moses. However, that He also used men as scribes for other messages on animal skins, parchment, or other materials such as paper is also understood. The Bible was written over a span of 1,500 years, by 40 authors. Unlike other religious writings, the Bible reads as a factual news account of real events, places, people, and dialogues. Historians and archaeologists have repeatedly confirmed its authenticity.

Using the authors' own writing styles and personalities, God shows us who He is and what it is like to know Him. It is "believed" by adherents that there is one central message consistently carried by all 40 chosen (canonized books) authors of the Bible: God, who created us all, desires a relationship with us. He calls us to know Him and trust Him.

Ardent users of the books believe that the Bible not only inspires us, it explains life and God to us. Whether the Bible answers all the questions we might have depends on where you are standing looking in. Believers say that the book teaches them how to live with purpose and compassion and how to relate to others. It encourages them to rely on God for strength, direction, and enjoy His love for mankind. The Bible also explains how we can have eternal life. Now, let us ask a side question. Does it follow that the users of the Bible could not make choices of good or bad on their own without following the recommendations in the Bible? How would they act if they suddenly stop using the Bible?

Some other claims include, but are not limited to:

There are multiple categories of evidence supporting the historical accuracy of the Bible as well as its claim to divine authorship.

That even where the Bible cannot be ascertained to have been dictated by God, there is the claim that it was perfectly guided and entirely inspired by Him.

As previously mentioned, humanly speaking, the Bible was written by approximately 40 men of diverse backgrounds over the course of

1,500 years. Isaiah was a prophet, Ezra was a priest, Matthew was a tax collector, John was a fisherman, Paul was a tentmaker, Moses was a shepherd, and Luke was a physician. According to believers, the Bible, despite being penned by different authors over 15 centuries, does not contradict itself and does not contain any errors. The authors all present different perspectives, but they all proclaim the same one God, and the same one way of salvation—Jesus Christ (John 3:16 and 14:6; Acts 4:12). Though few of the books of the Bible specifically name their author, below are the books of the Bible, along with the name of who is most assumed by biblical scholars to be the author, along with the approximate date of writing:

Genesis, Exodus, Leviticus, Numbers, and Deuteronomy	Moses	1400 BC
Joshua	Joshua	1350 BC
Judges, Ruth, 1 Samuel, 2 Samue	Unknown-	1000—900 BC
1 Kings, 2 Kings	Jeremiah	600 BC
1 Chronicles, 2 Chronicles, Ezra, Nehemiah	Ezra	450 BC
Esther	Mordecai	400 BC
Job	Unknown	- 1400 BC
Psalms	Various authors, and King David	1000–400 BC
Proverbs, Ecclesiastes, Song of Solomon	Solomon	900 BC
Isaiah	Isaiah	700 BC
Jeremiah, Lamentations	Jeremiah	- 600 BC
Ezekiel	Ezekiel	550 BC
Daniel	Daniel	550 BC
Hosea	Hosea	750 BC
Joel	Joel	850 BC
Amos	Amos	750 BC
Obadiah	Obadiah	600 BC
Jonah	Jonah	700 BC
Micah	Micah -	700 BC
Nahum	Nahum	650 BC
Habakkuk	Habakkuk -	600 BC
Zephaniah	Zephaniah	650 BC
Haggai	Haggai	520 BC
Zechariah	Zechariah	500 BC
Malachi	Malachi	430 BC
Matthew	Matthew	AD 55
Mark	John Mark	AD 50
Luke	Luke	AD 60
John	John	AD 90
Acts	Luke	AD 65
Romans, 1 Corinthians, 2 Corinthians, Galatians, Ephesians, Philippians	Paul	AD 50–70
Colossians, 1 Thessalonians, 2 Thessalonians	Paul	AD 50–70
1 Timothy, 2 Timothy, Titus, Philemon	Paul	AD 50–70
Hebrews	unknown, mostly likely Paul, Luke, Barnabas, or Apollos	AD 65
James	James	AD 45
1 Peter, 2 Peter	Peter	AD 60
1 John, 2 John, 3 John	John	AD 90
Jude	Jude	AD 60
Revelation	John	AD 90

There are many other books that were discarded and destroyed, for according to those who put the Bible together, those discarded books are not divine. Think about the book of the Prophet Enoch. If any book was to be judged as divine, the book of Enoch was it.

CHAPTER 6

Introduction to Science,
Doubts, and Faith

In the attempt to prove faith with science, one runs the risk of becoming a Thomas Didymus with attitude. I believe that faith is the believer's single most powerful argument for divine inspiration of scriptures, even as attempts to prove divine inspiration of scriptures show that the more you prove it, the less important faith becomes in the scheme of things. Hebrews 11:1 explains faith as being sure of what we hope for and certain of what we do not see. When you think about faith, you may think that there is/was an argument for faith that is presently unassailable by science. Something makes this argument immune from any kind of scientific criticism. What makes it immune is that there is no possible frame of reference from which the definition can be disproven. This analysis, however, is in keeping with the unchanging and perhaps unchangeable and fundamental qualities of scriptures that keep believers constrained to dogmas that must be upheld. To some, faith is the one unassailable proof of biblical inspiration. To others, understanding the processes of what otherwise would have been referred to as magic or faith is most likely to cement such faith, rather than faith built on a shaky foundation. Those who then seek to demonstrate the "inspired" take on the Bible with arguments and evidence are only trying to help build a stronger faith through confirmation reliant on empirical evidence.

There are instances where some would argue as if to lay a claim that science and scriptures are in total disagreement. That is so far from the truth. Some pretend like the scriptures do not aspire to such dynamic search for truth. This is because they believe that it is a static document that does not pretend to be a scientific treatise in the first place. Thus, it seems unnecessary to attempt to harmonize scripture with science.

The truth of the matter is that the Bible is full of scientific evidence. It has been so stated but most often our understanding and interpretations of such narratives is wanting. The Bible might seem static and unchanging in its narration of science, but science in itself, when established, is static. For example, that the earth rotates and revolves remains unchangeable and static. So, that we, as man, can prove this using science to harmonize with the Bible also gives our faith an increment in belief. Because of the many contradictions, contrasts, and confusion, there is a need to go further to harmonize scripture with science. The various religious groups will be doing a great disservice not to do so.

In one beautiful article I read, an opinion was expressed that *"While the Bible was not written as a science textbook, it is in harmony with true science when it deals with scientific matters. But other ancient books regarded as sacred contain scientific myths, inaccuracies, and outright falsehoods. Note just four of the many examples of the Bible's scientific accuracy:*

- *"How the earth is held in space." In ancient times when the Bible was being written, there was much speculation about how the earth was held in space. Some believed that the earth was supported by four elephants standing on a big sea turtle. Aristotle, a Greek philosopher and scientist of the fourth century BCE, taught that the earth could never hang in empty space. Instead, he taught that the heavenly bodies were fixed to the surface of solid, transparent spheres, with each sphere nested within another sphere. Supposedly the earth was on the innermost sphere, and the outermost sphere held the stars.*

Yet, rather than reflect the fanciful, unscientific views existing at the time of its writing, the Bible simply stated (in about the year 1473 BCE): "[God is] hanging the earth upon nothing (Job 26:7)." In the original Hebrew, the word for "nothing" used here means "not anything," and this is the only time it occurs in the Bible. The picture it presents of an earth surrounded by empty space is recognized by scholars as a remarkable vision for its time. The Theological Wordbook of the Old Testament says: "Job 26:7 strikingly pictures the then-known world as suspended in space, thereby anticipating future scientific discovery."

The Bible's accurate statement predated Aristotle by over 1,100 years. Yet, Aristotle's views continued to be taught as fact for some 2,000 years after his death! Finally, in 1687 CE, Sir Isaac Newton published his findings that the earth was held in space in relation to other heavenly objects by mutual attraction, that is, gravity. But that was close to 3,200 years after the Bible had stated with elegant simplicity that the earth is hanging "upon nothing."

Yes, nearly 3,500 years ago, the Bible correctly noted that the earth has no visible support, a fact that is in harmony with the more recently understood laws of gravity and motion. "How Job knew the truth," said one scholar, "is a question not easily solved by those who deny the inspiration of Holy Scripture."

• *"The shape of the earth." The Encyclopedia Americana said: "The earliest known image that men had of the earth was that it was a flat, rigid platform at the center of the universe . . . The concept of a spherical earth was not widely accepted until the Renaissance." Some early navigators even feared that they might sail off the edge of the flat earth. Then the introduction of the compass and other advancements made possible longer ocean voyages. These "voyages of discovery," another encyclopedia explains, "showed that the world was round, not flat as most people had believed."*

Yet, long before such voyages, about 2,700 years ago, the Bible said: "There is One who is dwelling above the circle of the earth" (Isaiah 40:22). The Hebrew word here translated "circle" can also mean "sphere," as various reference works note. Other Bible translations, therefore, say, "the globe of the earth" (Douay Version) and "the round earth," Moffatt.

*Some insist on interpreting this as a "flat circular earth," as a disc or pie. Since that was the concept used by mankind at the time the Bible was written, one could also accept that interpretation. Note, though, that one's interpretation today of such information does not mandate that this be the **only** interpretation, as noted above.*

Thus, the Bible was not influenced by the unscientific views prevalent at the time regarding the earth's support and its shape. The reason is simple: The Author of the Bible is the Author of the universe. He created the earth, so He should know what it hangs on and what its shape is. Hence, when He inspired the Bible, He saw to it that no unscientific views were incorporated in it, however much they may have been believed by others at the time.

• *"The composition of living things." "Jehovah God proceeded to form the man out of dust from the ground" Genesis 2:7 states. The World Book Encyclopedia says: "All the chemical elements that make up living things are also present in nonliving matter." So all the basic chemicals that make up living organisms, including man, are also found in the earth itself. This harmonizes with the*

Bible's statement that identifies the material God used in creating humans and all other living things.

- *"According to their kinds." The Bible states that God created the first human pair and that from them all other humans descended (Genesis 1:26–28, 3:20). It says that other living things, such as fish, birds, and mammals, did the same, coming forth "according to their kinds" (Genesis 1:11, 12, 21, 24, 25). This is just what scientists have found in the natural creation, that every living thing comes from a parent of like kind. There is no exception. In this regard, physicist Raymo observes: "Life makes life; it happens all the time in every cell. But how did non-life make life?" It is one of the biggest unanswered questions in biology, and so far, biologists can offer little more than wild guesses. Somehow, inanimate matter managed to get itself organized in an animate way. . . . The author of Genesis may have had it right, after all (Wiki.answers).*

I am very sure that I do not have an adequate vocabulary to pay the above description the needed compliments. Let us seek to understand what divinely inspired actually means. I am of the understanding that when interpreters of the book speak of the Bible as inspired, they are referring to a belief that God divinely influenced the human authors of the scriptures in such a way that what they wrote was the very Word of God. In this context of the scriptures, the word *inspiration* simply means "God-breathed." Inspiration, therefore, means that the Bible truly is the Word of God and makes the Bible unique among all other books. This explanation is very important because if one God spoke the words, there could be no confusion associated with the message.

Divine, according to the Thesaurus dictionary, means heavenly, celestial, godly, great, marvelous, neat, etc. It is interesting that one of the words used to explain divine is "discover." *Discover* means to guess, presume, deduce, discern, and perceive. It is very telling how divine had to be explained away as to "discover." However, the bigger question is, "Did the Bible claim to be divinely inspired or was that claim made by promoters of the Bible?" According to a group, the Catholic Answers, "No book of the Bible claims itself to be divinely inspired. Divine inspiration means that God himself authored the exact words of the text (using the human writer's mind, personality, and background), and no book states anything like, 'The words of this book were chosen by God' or 'This book is divinely inspired.'"

The term *inspired* only occurs once in the Bible (2 Timothy 3:16), where we are told that all scripture is inspired. The thinking is that of knowing that something is scripture, and then we infer that it is inspired. The point is that we do not initially conclude that it is inspired before inferring that it is scripture.

At times, we find that when references to inspiration occur, it is when one book of the Bible reports that God, or the Spirit, spoke through the words of a different book. For instance, see Hebrews 3:7–11, concerning Psalm 95. In no case does a book of the Bible state this for itself except in specific instances in the Old Testament as a directive to Moses. In such instances, it was for a specific recording of an event. Even if it does claim to contain divine revelations just like in the book of Revelation, it does not say of itself that every word of its text was inspired. Most often, the inference to inspiration is based on New Testament reference to the Old Testament. In one instance, the book of Prophet Enoch, a book not included in the Bible, was mentioned approximately two times in the New Testament (Jude verse 14). That is something we must infer from 2 Timothy 3:16.

All scripture is given by inspiration of God and is profitable for doctrine, for reproof, for correction. Since no protocanonical book of the Bible meets this test, it can hardly be expected of the deuterocanonical books.

Thus, the claim of inspiration is a different thing from really being inspired. When we read the Epistle of Jude quoting Prophet Enoch's "inspired" words, thus justifying the claims of being the Word of God, you may wonder why the book was omitted from the Bible. This brings to question the meaning of inspiration and how it was applied to the selection of the books that made up the inspired words of the books of the Bible. However, the theologians have since concluded the divine inspiration of the Bible.

Because the scriptures are the inspired Word of God, we can conclude that they are also inerrant and authoritative. Most readers of the Holy Book have concluded that because it is divine, there are no mistakes, confusions, and deception. But, what if there is confusion in the Bible? Would that render the Book no longer divine? Would those conflicts and resulting confusion render the Holy Bible no longer inerrant and authoritative? It is the intention of this writer to let the Bible stand on its own two feet, so to speak, and discount those characterizations that make the Bible what it was not. Many times and in places where you expect to hear the truth you hear people alluding to the Bible's text in ways that the Bible never intended. As we now move into the body of the Bible we will show with biblical evidence some instances where confusion, misinterpretations, and misrepresentations have jumbled the integrity of the Holy Book.

Meanwhile, let us seriously and logically look at the Pentateuch, the five books credited to Moses. The first thing that pops up in one's mind is the recording of the death of Moses. That is a whopper of a giveaway. Even the nonanalytical mind can see through this if the scales of indoctrination have not beclouded the mind. How Moses achieved this feat is beyond imagination, but, of course, that alone is a clincher that Moses, even if he wrote part of the Pentateuch, cannot lay claim to all the works in the Pentateuch. It would have been more logical if the writer(s) claimed that the recording of Moses' death was divinely recorded as was Moses' burial. Whether the followers of the book, the Bible, are stubbornly dismissive about this big mistake is beyond me. If such a mistake was made in Deuteronomy, what other mistakes may have been made in other books and remain unfound?

What the recording of the death of Moses proved was that the book of Deuteronomy, like many of the Bible's books, was written in stages and by different authors living in different historical eras. Though this is true, the book, Deuteronomy, displays a remarkable unity in its style, theology, narrative, and message so much so that most theologians and clergy fail to see that the book was a narrative set and written within various eras and by different authors. There were, however, mentions of Moses being instructed to write as in Exodus 17:14, 24:4, and 34:27. In all those circumstances, Moses was instructed to write on specific issues. That does not amount to a confirmation that Moses wrote the five books. When read and studied properly, the book of Deuteronomy has post-Mosaic events. It also has late monarchal and exile periods in it. There is strong evidence from the biblical texts themselves for a pre-Mosaic era, a post-Mosaic era, late monarchal, and even exilic dates for the composition of much of this Old Testament narrative, especially the book of Deuteronomy whose date of composition has unanimously been shown to be approximately in the seventh century BC, under King Josiah's reign. In other words, if a reader of a narrative reads a text where iPhones, high-definition (HD) televisions, and mobile phones were mentioned and later archaeologically discovered, it gives a clue as to what era the writing may have taken place, for it is impossible for those items to be mentioned in a narrative set in the era of 1900s.

Like all the books that made up the Bible, the propaganda that the text was somehow divinely inspired is itself an interpretative spin that got formed from the theological, ideological, and even polemical perspectives of those who put the book together. This type of thinking is already embedded in theological interpretations, or misinterpretations, that easily resonate with a priori assumption; after all, we are talking about a canonical text here—a book doctored by a few "inspired men."

As we have seen, some accepted writings of yesteryears of events like the "stars coming to a standstill" will be laughed off by today's scientifically inclined. I am not a scientist, but my little understanding of scientific concepts makes the narrative of stars coming to a standstill laughable. Certain recorded events in the Holy Book cannot survive when science concepts are applied. However, science and logic must not allow stupidity to take hold because science cannot survive new stupidities that may arise. Nothing can survive against stupidity, because stupidity is the most ineffective weapon against everything rational. Stupidity is when a grown man picks up and holds a rattlesnake believing that by faith he has control over serpents because he read a verse in the Gospel of Matthew that seemingly suggests that. Obviously, common sense had jumped out of the window of reason. By the way, many faithful believers have met untimely death practicing this.

Man has come a long way. Man has come from primitivism in the ancient times to today's level of development, and he continues the attempts at avoiding conflicts of religion. While many countries have attempted to avoid conflict by separating religion and state from each other, some have opined whether religion and science are really diametrically opposed to each other. As science continues to explain what hitherto were miracles, religionists amend their strongly held position to reinterpret and reinvent to explain and understand nature and the physical world. As the influence of science continues to dog previously held religious doctrines, different religions have dealt with it differently.

Can religious dogma and its inherent confusion survive in the face of science and logic, or is it doomed to the surfacing evidence revealing the workings of nature and/or the Almighty Universal Creator whose name we do not know?

The Bible is full of contradictions and inconsistencies. The Bible's purpose is to teach salvation, but those who subscribe to the Book have made the Book more than the simple historical documentation that it really is. They have wrapped the Book with divine and other descriptions. It is therefore not a mistake if people make the mistake of considering it a treatise on science, history, and other interpretations. Though many have dispensed with the necessity of a Creator(s), this writer does not subscribe to the notion that some scientific experiments and/or theories could dispense with the concept of creation. That position was critically discussed in the book *Why Was Man Created?*

Let me make it clear that it is indeed possible for me to accept other viewpoints, as long as they are evidentially supported and logically conceived. I am a Bible-believing Catholic like many, but have since started seriously examining other points of view. As a result, I learned what objective scholars have discovered about the Bible's origins, and some of its convoluted developmental history. Reading through the Bible and critically analyzing and plotting and connecting the dots, I have come to have exposure to and understanding of the Bible's various shocking inconsistencies and contradictions. These, among others, helped shape my viewpoint. Also, having been exposed to other rationalizations filled with everything irrational except logic and common sense, I have come to the realization that biblical accounts often conflict with well-corroborated scientific evidence, which further contributed to my transition to a more enlightened and logical viewpoint. In this work, my statements express solely my opinions and/or beliefs and do not in any way represent those of any of my preachers whom I had listened to over the years. Approximately 99.99 percent of them know no better, for why must an enlightened person waste time to listen to a preacher say that the earth is 6,000 years old?

My fascination with this work is the interpretations, or misinterpretations, of the Bible. Can you imagine how great it would be if the Bible's texts are left alone to stand as is? This is therefore also a plea to let the Bible find its voice. It is a plea to let the Bible stand as is. This book is the most recent expression of interpretations of Bible texts that were reached in my series of books, including *Why Was Man Created?* that explored the questionable claims of evolutionists and creationists.

As in my other books, I attempt to give a fuller treatment to both the positive and negative aspects of letting the Bible stand as is. I am well aware of traditional interpretations given to Bible stories. In some cases, the conjuring of mostly imagined imagery to suit and give theological themes is frowned at. New and simple logical interpretation of narratives is arrived at by just letting the Bible stand as is. Applying logic and common sense is the critically analytical tool here. Conjuring images is likened to offering evidences not related to a case. It is a slippery slope.

Against this backdrop of exclusion and inclusion of nonexistent imagery to create a particular dogma, we analyze employing a modern-day level of development and juxtapose into historic details that help open up a clearer understanding of characters and events. Though this is by no means an attempt on our part at rewriting the biblical narrative, we allow every involved story used in this work to retain their original context and text. This approach may be challenging for some because they might be reluctant to analyze closely the biblical texts for fear that they will "offend" God while putting aside critical analysis that should broaden and expand our understanding of the recorded historical happenings of that time.

Now, let us consider some misinterpretations and confusions . . . but before, that let us consider the Writer of the Bible—God Himself.

CHAPTER 7

Confusion: Many Routes to God(s)?

As a child, I often accompanied my immediate and extended families to their religious outings. I listened to their conversations and practices. My extended family exposed me to various practices of Christianity and

Islam. Some had no practices because they are nonreligious, and then there are those who served God by calling on various channels to reach Him—the animists. Yet, in all of these practices, you can notice the desire for and reverence of a Supreme Being. The practice is to supplicate the Supreme Being via smaller intermediaries. I recall an incident when I was in the company of an uncle during a religious ceremony. An animal offering was required. I watched the slaughter of the animal . . . and I passed out. I knew I passed out because I was told. However, the experiences of these folks communicating to reach God(s) were not lost on me.

Different members of society contact God through various means. Christians have their means. Muslims have their ways. Animists have their paths. Buddhists have their means and so do other religions. These varied means to contact or communicate with the divine in itself is confusing as no one means can lay claim to be the best communicative highway route to God. Some pass their message through a tree which they believe has a spiritual soul. Others do so through some type of animals and/or waters. Is it not interesting that our forefathers knew that trees had a soul in them? They knew nothing about DNA, yet they knew that the trees are alive with a soul. All living creations have a direct connection to DNA. Scientists would tell you that—although speaking as a layman, the concentration of man's DNA is greater than that of animals and trees. Is it not surprising that man's concentration of DNA is approximately 1 percent more than that of a chimpanzee?

The issue described above is a demonstration by individuals in different and the same societies of how to worship God(s) as they deem fit and as they understand. Whether they are doing it right is an answer someone who goes to God through another means cannot provide. Every society makes supplications on behalf of themselves and society to a god or gods they understand would protect their interest. These interests could be farming, fishing, and/or war. The Jewish God, after all, was a god of war.

Some may simply, with a wave of the hand, diminish and dismiss the significance of animism and its connotation as described above but the take away from animism is its practice and belief in polytheist beings—what archaeologists are finding out today. These polytheist gods blessed their worshippers according to their area of specialty. Thus, you had gods for fertility, rain, iron, war, etc. So also did the biblical Yahweh promise to do things for the Jews in exchange for worship in ways He demanded. These demands are documented in the covenants.

In perspective, I learned that God is kind if you did good deeds. God is merciful, and God protects, for He is good. So we are told. I also learned that God is cruel and unmerciful. For example, the animist taught that if you covet your neighbors' belongings and the owner sought punishment for the thief, god goes after the thief immediately and the consequence is death. When such punishment was delivered by the gods, the dead man's properties are then confiscated and dumped near the house of the god that inflicted the judgment. In societies where such practice is existent, worshippers shy away from bad deeds for fear they could be struck dead. To some, it is all superstition; to others, it is religion. This is confusion at its best—albeit nonbiblical. But that was then.

As a young adult and a practicing Christian, my take on God was that of a monotheistic being; forgiving, merciful and kind; a comforter, deliverer, and conqueror of enemies; protector and one who we go to in life hereafter or thereafter. The very first thing one was taught to grasp is how good and merciful God really is. So, the first things we will need to grasp from scripture are the specific verses that portray how merciful, kind, and compassionate God the Father really is. We are indoctrinated to accept that if we do not believe that God the Father is a good, merciful, loving, kind, and compassionate God—then we would not be able to receive a divine healing from Him because we do not have enough faith and belief in His ability to even want to heal us in the first place. To that extent, some even prefer prayers to prescription medicine. It is confusion galore.

It seems that those that laid the framework to select the books that made up the Bible already knew this, so the first thing each Christian is taught is a belief by faith. I am sure that I am not the first, neither will I be the last, to bore you with these tales, but when something ails one, the best reaction is to find solutions to what ails you. To this end, I devoted time to study the book. When I say time, I mean *serious* time—not like setting-an-hour-aside-here-and-an-hour-there kind of time.

I listened to interpreters and preachers talk of the various holy books. Some parts are not rational. I wanted more. I was not accepting these diverse interpretations or misinterpretations from various deliveries of the message. The confusion was becoming unbearable. I started reading the books on my own. So, below, let us look at this table and compare and contrast a few of God's qualities of the Christian and Jewish faith.

How merciful is God?

God is kind, merciful, and good.	*God is cruel, unmerciful, and evil.*
Exodus 34:6 The LORD God, merciful and gracious, longsuffering, and abundant in goodness and truth.	Exodus 34:6–7 The Lord God . . . visiting the iniquity of the fathers upon the children, and upon the children's children, unto the third and to the fourth generation.
Deuteronomy 4:31 For the Lord thy God is a merciful God.	Numbers 25:4 And the Lord said to Moses, Take all the heads of the people, and hang them up before the Lord against the sun, that the fierce anger of the Lord may be turned away from Israel.
2 Samuel 24:14 Let us fall now into the hand of the LORD; for his mercies are great.	
1 Chronicles 16:34; Psalm 106:1, 107:1, 118:1, 136:1 O give thanks unto the Lord; for he is good; for his mercy endureth forever.	Deuteronomy 7:16 And thou shalt consume all the people which the Lord thy God shall deliver thee; thine eye shall have no pity upon them.
Psalm 25:8 Good and upright is the Lord.	1 Samuel 6:19 Because they had looked into the ark of the Lord, even he smote of the people fifty thousand, and three score and ten men.

How merciful is God? (cont.)

God is kind, merciful, and good.

Psalm 86:5
For thou, Lord, art good, and ready to forgive; and plenteous in mercy unto all them that call upon thee.

Psalm 100:5
For the Lord is good, his mercy is everlasting.

Psalm 103:8
The Lord is merciful and gracious, slow to anger, and plenteous in mercy.

Psalm 145:9
The Lord is good to all, and his tender mercies are over all his works.

Jeremiah 3:12
I will not cause mine anger to fall upon you: for I am merciful, saith the LORD, and I will not keep anger forever.

Jeremiah 33:11
The LORD is good; for his mercy endureth forever.

Lamentations 3:33
For he doth not afflict willingly nor grieve the children of men.

Joel 2:13
For he is gracious and merciful, slow to anger, and of great kindness.

Micah 7:18
Who is a God like unto thee, that pardoneth iniquity, and passeth by the transgression of the remnant of his heritage? he retaineth not his anger for ever, because he delighteth in mercy.

God is cruel, unmerciful, and evil.

1 Samuel 15:2–3
Now go and smite Amalek, and utterly destroy all that they have, and spare them not, but slay both man and woman, infant and suckling.

Lamentation 2:2
The LORD hath swallowed up all the habitations of Jacob, and hath not pitied.

Lamentations 2:17
The LORD hath done that which he had devised . . . He hath thrown down, and hath not pitied.

Lamentations 3:43
Thou hast slain, thou hast not pitied.

Jeremiah 13:14
I will not pity, nor spare, nor have mercy, but destroy.

Jeremiah 16:3–7
For thus saith the LORD concerning the sons and concerning the daughters that are born in this place, and concerning their mothers that bare them, and concerning their fathers that begat them in this land; They shall die of grievous deaths; they shall not be lamented; neither shall they be buried; but they shall be as dung upon the face of the earth: and they shall be consumed by the sword, and by famine; and their carcases shall be meat for the fowls of heaven, and for the beasts of the earth. For thus saith the LORD, Enter not into the house of mourning, neither go to lament nor bemoan them: for I have taken away my peace from this people, saith the LORD, even loving kindness and mercies. Both the great and the small shall

How merciful is God? (cont.)

God is kind, merciful, and good.	God is cruel, unmerciful, and evil.
Judith 13:21 Give all of you glory to him, because he is good, because his mercy endureth for ever. 2 Corinthians 1:3 Blessed be God . . . the Father of mercies. James 5:11 For the Lord is very pitiful and of tender mercy. 1 John 4:16 God is love.	die in this land: they shall not be buried, neither shall men lament for them, nor cut themselves, nor make themselves bald for them: Neither shall men tear themselves for them in mourning, to comfort them for the dead; neither shall men give them the cup of consolation to drink for their father or for their mother. Ezekiel 7:4, 9 And mine eye shall not spare thee, neither will I have pity. Ezekiel 9:5–6 Go ye after him through the city, and smite: let not your eye spare, neither have ye pity: Slay utterly old and young, both maids, and little children, and women. Micah 1:12 But evil came down from the LORD unto the gate of Jerusalem.

Credit for the above table: http://skepticsannotatedbible.com/contra/merciful.html

If the ability to study, understand, and respond to difficult subjects is one of the greatest joys and excitement, then the ability and opportunity to communicate that hard-won puzzle to others is a very close second. Having experienced the power of excitement of decoding the narration through understanding and application of common sense and logic, there is always a contagious desire to share that with others. The point is to help you share in the unraveling of the scripture with greater skill, understanding, and enjoyment. When you deconstruct a confusing text you have a feeling like I had of moving from understanding a text of scripture which was once misinterpreted, to communicating that unraveled text of scripture. It feels good when it all makes sense. It makes your understanding clear, your belief hinged on rock, and your worship effortless.

CHAPTER 8

Losing Faith?

I have come across religionists who confess that they are confused. That they daily question their beliefs as learned from the Bible. To these folks, I simply recommend the book *Why Was Man Created?* Regarding these folks, I still find the basic tenets of their faith doubtful, so rather than stay and explain some more, I simply recommend a book that is packed with evidence that confirms the existence of not just that God they believe in, but of the existence of gods. I have had some express thanks in the process. As for me, belief in the biblical Yahweh is a foregone conclusion. In the Bible He exists. I repeat: He exists.

For many years I have gone round and round with many religionists on what amounts to one central topic: the morality of dogmatic religious teachings. When you listen to many of them who wear religion on their sleeves, you hear their many years of worthless musings and often tortured ramblings. They have repeated these musings and ramblings over and over so many times, they believe their preachments to be true. You feel sorry for them for you know that years of doubt have wrecked, and are still wrecking, serious havoc on their tortured minds.

There are, however, both honest and dishonest reasons for people giving up on God, and there are remedies for both.

Some of the most common honest reasons I have cited for people losing faith is that it becomes impossible to believe in a God that is defined as being simultaneously all-powerful and all-loving and omnipresent and immutable when believers in that God were/are tortured and killed. And, sometimes the God leading the killing is the God they are supposed to believe in. The message I take here is the confirmation of this God but not necessarily His behavior while protecting His people. He is, after all, the God of war. Though, there are those who as always would come up with rationalizations to justify all the inadequacies of this God, such rationalizations do not help remove these doubts and confusions; instead, it helps to solidify the doubts and confusions.

There are times when certain things happen, believers stand confused and ask, "God, where are you?" That question is the one asked in the pinnacle of doubts and confusion. It is however a very good question. It is equally as logical as it is reasonable because it digs deep into the preached omnipresence of this God.

Let us reason this: All of these questions arise from one basic fallacy and that is that God is simultaneously loving and infinitely powerful. Strangely enough, most Christians believe that both of those assertions are true even though reality states otherwise. There are those who will call this heresy, but there is little question that the God who is incarnated in Jesus Christ is a God who is not all-powerful because if He is the same God, He is a God who has given up power in order to express His love. And that is the portrayal in the Gospels. Thoughtful, reasonable, and logical reflection would lead anyone to understand that it is impossible to express and exercise love and power at the same time.

My question to you, the reader, is this: When does the doubt or nonbelief go away? Will there ever be a time where you will actually wholeheartedly believe in God? At times, does it feel like you believe in God on a good day but question His existence at other times? But even on those good days, it only feels like you took comfort in the prospect of God's existence, but then it's not that you actually believe in Him. Some people are confused. They want to believe in God more than anything. Sometimes they ask, "What happens if God does not exist?" To some, belief is a balancing game. It is as if some people are in a balance of belief and nonbelief, tipping back and forth as the seasons of events go by. I had a friend with whom I attended church services in those days. We were young. It was as if we were in competition to see who believed in God the most. It got frustrating. It got frustrating for me because it was pretense on my part. It was pretense because I believed by faith. Faith was like being led by the nose. I hate that and will ever hate that. I was now telling my friend that one of the things that keeps me going through this struggle is the anticipation of superior information in the future. In the future I see myself believing in God and raising a family with that belief and conviction. I decided that it is something I would not give up on. I will not settle for nonbelief. I will not settle for belief through faith either. I must find evidence for what I believe as I do not want to be pretending to believe in God that others made up for me while they believed by faith.

The prevailing circumstance was one of theological rationalism sometimes called evidentialism—a view that faith, in order to be rational, must be based on sound logic and evidence. I have met people who in the attempt to flaunt their belief touted doubt as a virtue of mature religious life, and believers were supposed to follow unflinchingly the demands of faith wherever it might lead. According to such believers, the secret to dealing with doubt in the religious life is not to resolve all of one's doubts. They pacify our doubts by suggesting more doubts as in "One will always have unanswered questions." They suggest that the secret to faith is learning to live victoriously with the unanswered questions. Some preachers go so far as advising one to be in tune with a "true foundation of faith" so that when logic and evidence cannot answer our questions, a mind built on the true foundation of faith will prevent unanswered questions from turning into destructive doubts. That some questions are unanswerable was the motivating factor for my first book *Why Was Man Created?* Faith is a conviction that what you believe is true. Conviction comes by knowing, learning, and observing. This is how a foundation of truth is built. Now, what then is the true foundation of faith? How can you build a foundation from nothing? This is one of the many reasons people have doubts. But there are evidences that can build one's belief. All you need to do is find the evidence.

Any thinking religious person will have a box filled with questions of unresolved doubts. What a reasonable person is expected to do is resolve the doubts by answering the nagging questions through research. For me, I can safely say that working hard on my unresolved questions and finding answers that satisfied me intellectually, logically, and reasonably is one of the most exhilarating experiences for a believer and/or nonbeliever. To resolve a doubt that has troubled you for a long time brings a tremendously wonderful sense of intellectual satisfaction and inspiration. Such inspiration brings confidence that, one by one, the other nagging questions of doubt will have solutions.

Whenever I had questions that shook my belief or nonbelief about a particular issue, I usually set aside some time to study that specific issue by researching it. One thing you should never do is sit and drown in your ocean of doubts. Because of some doubts I had, I had to keep after such doubts until I ran them aground. You can do the same. There are so many misconceptions about why people lose faith in religion that I thought I would write a book about why I lost faith and found evidence. Yet, in order to explain my loss of faith I have to explain also that I found evidence. Lots of evidence.

I found that the Bible, though, has its difficulty in narratives, but the biggest issue was in the interpretation of the book. Such misrepresentations through misinterpretations are among some reasons why many believers became atheists. There are some common misconceptions about why people are atheists. We will have to address some of those here. Many people did not become atheists because they hate God. Not believing in something doesn't mean that you hate it. And how can one hate something one believes to be nonexistent? The religion, Christianity and others, and their followers, have not done something so horrible to atheists that made an atheist give up faith in disgust. Oftentimes, it is the insistency that people believe by faith that drives people into atheism. There are good people, religious people. There are evil religious people too.

The reason that many lose their faith is ultimately because a religion creates confusion due to varying interpretations and misinterpretations. It is contradictory, and some people, after reading the books of the Bible, have come to the conclusion that the God of the Bible is cruel. I cannot fault the writers of the books which comprised the Bible for their chosen narrating style in which they described the events they experienced and witnessed because they lacked the vocabulary to describe what they saw. They just described what they saw in the best possible available words they could come up with. But describe what they saw, they did. That there is confusion in understanding and/or interpreting what they left for us as the historical documentation of events at that time is something we must decode and solve for posterity. This book, therefore, is an attempt at decoding important biblical texts that would make you view the Bible in a different light. As I write what would ordinarily be considered unpalatable to some in certain places, facts cannot be silenced, and facts, even in the face of anticipated evaluations, stand tall and conquer all lies for there is truly no such thing as blasphemy—a word coined and decided on by persons who are already insanely drunk from the bottles of indoctrination. Indoctrination incapacitates free thought.

CHAPTER 9

Free Will

The greatest gift the creators gave to you and me is the ability to free think. Free thought, therefore, is the greatest gift you can give back to the creators by exercising freewill. Freewill is the ability of individuals to make choices unconstrained by certain factors like organized religion. The reason the creators gave you free thought is so that you would have the ability to reason for self, to grow and advance and grow some more. In fact, the creators were so satisfied when man started using his mind to advance self. The Bible states in Genesis 11:1–6:

11 And the whole earth was of one language, and of one speech.

[2] And it came to pass, as they journeyed from the east, that they found a plain in the land of Shinar, and they dwelt there.

[3] And they said one to another, "Come, let us make bricks and burn them thoroughly." And they had brick for stone, and slime had they for mortar.

[4] And they said, "Come, let us build us a city and a tower whose top may reach unto heaven; and let us make us a name, lest we be scattered abroad upon the face of the whole earth."

⁵ And the Lord came down to see the city and the tower which the children of men built.

⁶ And the Lord said, ***"Behold, the people are one and they have all one language, and this they begin to do; and now nothing will be withheld from them which they have imagined to do."***

If God gave us the capacity to think and reason, then why would He hold it against us to use that tool and ask good, hard questions about faith? Irrespective and regardless of what exists beyond our planet, do we think or fear that a Supreme Being is going to banish a soul for eternity for simply embracing the gift of freethinking? Free thought is a philosophical viewpoint that holds opinions which should be formed on the basis of logic, reason, and empiricism, rather than authority, tradition, or other dogmas gained through indoctrination. The cognitive application of free thought is known as *freethinking*, and practitioners of free thought are known as *freethinkers*. However, unless certainty is certain, no one should boast to be a freethinker, because truth is the only thing that is truly true, for if we claim we have more truth than the generations of the past, we must be able to disprove the generations of the past to a large extent. It is not enough for the freethinkers to perceive to be free from the bondage of superstition of religious beliefs, but that the freethinker has come to a rational knowledge of reality instead of believing in things on the basis of faith. So, for me, I do not claim nonexistence of beings that are superintelligent with a governing hierarchy at the top of which there is a deity that mankind refers to as God. After all, the best of us cannot find happiness in ignorance.

A mind is unique because it can come up with an infinity of ideas, for it can be used to think about almost anything in a thousand different ways. Therefore, any act that deliberately confines a mind to a singular way of observing things cannot be acting for all the potential good there may be.

It can be quite easy to fall to the temptation to do what everyone else is doing and to start thinking what others believe in. Most often, with cliques, subcultures, political parties, and movements, you can easily give up your own identity for a collective. You, therefore, subordinate your ideas for the group's ideas. Thus, you start engaging in group-think. Of course, this is not necessary as one can still retain individuality. Group-think may be good as a concept, but most often, group-think is commandeered and applied in such a way that its products are devastating. In some societies, especially developing ones, group-think can be a tool to rally a community/ peoples into avoidable confrontation with another community/peoples. Group-think is someone who is a people pleaser. There is nothing wrong with attempting to be nice and sociable, but you should not have to do anything that violates your best interest or moral code merely for others. If you dress, act, socialize, or make decisions in a certain way so that you fit in to please others, you are a good group-think person. This is not to say there are no situations where and when we have to group-think for to do otherwise could either be stupid or ignorant or both.

In the same way a man can be chained to an iron railing in a police cell, a mind can be chained to an assumption, a religion, or any idea of any kind. To therefore allow self to be indoctrinated to dogmas is to limit the mind, to mankind's disadvantage. That is why we must ask questions to understand because the beginning of wisdom starts with asking questions. Why do we believe what we believe? And how do we know what we know? To some, indoctrination in religions has become a chain. They have been chained and padlocked to a stationery iron railing. The troubling aspect though is that they do not know that they have been chained. Many of history's great leaders chose to ask questions—lots of questions. Some stepped away from the norms and cultures of the time to free themselves from conventions and commitments of normal life. Only then were they able to learn, discovered, transformed, and understood things in ways that ultimately changed the earth.

Today, some are still chained to shackles of doctrines of some philosophers or a political party or by the heaviest chain of them all—religion.

Would your religion allow you to use and exercise this gift of free thought? Religion, as we know, is an organized collection of beliefs and cultural systems that relate humanity to an order of existence. Most religions have narratives and symbols that are intended to explain the meaning and purpose of life. These explanations vary from religion to religion, sect to sect, and usually meanings depend on who is doing the interpretation, or misinterpretation, as the case may be.

As one who would not allow Bible interpreters to bully me into group-think, I will here let you in on one Bible verse and interpret it to your dismay. This verse tells of the Gods landing on earth. Below, I use four different versions of the Bible.

KJV (online), Genesis 1:2: And the earth was without form and void, and darkness was upon the face of the deep. **And the Spirit of God moved upon the face of the waters.**

NIV, Genesis 1:2: Now the earth was formless and empty, darkness was over the surface of the deep, **and the Spirit of God was hovering over the waters.**

NAS, Genesis 1:2: The earth was formless and void, and darkness was over the surface of the deep, and the Spirit of God was moving over the surface of the waters.

International Standard Version, Genesis 1:2: When the earth was as yet unformed and desolate, with the surface of the ocean depths shrouded in darkness, **and while the Spirit of God was hovering over the surface of the waters . . .**

If an everyday Bible reader is asked what the above means, they are likely to say: The Spirit of the Lord or God's Spirit was omnipresent and moving around the waters. But that is an ignorant interpretation and that is one of the reasons misinterpretations have created more disbelievers than believers. That is very far from the meaning of that verse. It is interesting that who or whatever dictated that part of Genesis had nothing to hide as they told the story as it really happened. In verse one, they started with "In the beginning God created the heaven and the earth . . ."

AND quickly moved to explain God's arrival and mode of arrival on earth; thus, in verse two, "and the spirit of God hovered upon the face of the waters."

> ² And the earth was without form and void, and darkness was upon the face of the deep. And the Spirit of God moved upon the face of the waters.

That verse 2, alone, if understood, puts the argument to rest that there is no God. It also describes the form of transportation and arrival of these God(s) via an aircraft christened "Spirit of God" that hovered on the surface of the waters as there was no dry land to land upon. That verse, if understood, puts to rest the argument that there were no intelligent beings. That verse confirms that there were intelligent beings existing long before the earth formed. The name of the Gods' aircraft will come into play again in the book of Prophet Ezekiel, and is described again in the book of Enoch. Do not forget that science puts earth's age at 4.6 billion years and 13.7 billion for the universe. What this means is that there were intelligent beings billions of years ago before earth formed. It is therefore wise to logically assume that their knowledge and experience far exceeds our still developing intelligence, discoveries, and experience. It is also logical to assume that if man was to live just 4.6 billion years, our intelligence, discoveries, and experiences will far outpace the level where we are at this moment.

Genesis verse two, therefore, is a description of the initial moments when the intelligent beings landed on earth's atmosphere. And the whole earth was covered in water and the Spirit of God (i.e., aircraft) hovered on the surface of the water. That is all there is about that. At this juncture, I must ask you to read the book God Is Not Enough, Messiah Needed *to get the full details of the Lord's spacecrafts, jets, and helicopters. We will, however, no matter how brief, explain biblical aircrafts in later chapters in this work.*

CHAPTER 10

Misinterpretation Fuels Confusion

It is assumed by many that biblical narratives are *indirect* in the way they communicate their message. It is also assumed that such narratives appeal primarily to the senses, not so much to the intellect directly as expositional writing does. This assumption is perhaps the reason many Bible-thumpers see mountains where there is a valley and see the trait of omnipresence where God's mode of travel could not be explained.

Because of the above assumptions, any preacher can invite you into "their" biblical world of characters and experiences. They invite you to see what they believe they see. They construct in their minds images plucked from anywhere but the Bible. Their new divine world is built on settings, characters, and plots, usually involving conflict and doom, tests, and the desire to look spiritually wise. Such settings hardly have the meaning of what the Bible conveyed. They make the Bible seem more difficult than it really is. This, often, becomes confusing as one setting might mean many things to different teachers. When a narrative is explained, we must open up our listeners to the world of the stories by taking the time to create a *setting* in such a way that our listeners feel transported into the world of the story. In this attempt to create an imagined take of a narrative, interpreters must see a need for the creative and fertile use of imagination to enable parishioners smell the sea breeze, hear the sounds of children crying, and see the lame man jump for joy, as it were. You, therefore, help your people enter into the lives and struggles/victories of the characters you have painted for them.

The bottom line is that there is always confusion in interpretations when reading, decoding, and teaching a story from the Bible. It would help to place the listeners into the story's setting and make them identify with the characters in the story. It would help to let the audience live the story, as if they were there when it happened. However, an audience can only relive these experiences as the preacher experienced it. Thus, *re-creation of the truth* is of the essence in teaching narrative material. For example, if we read the book of Ezekiel 10:1–9 quoted below, you will see that my take on the meaning of these verses are totally at odds with that of a religious take. For me, I see nothing religious or spiritual here, whereas some see Israel, Jerusalem, destruction, God, and Moses. My take is a total deviation from others'. My take is true and logical, though drastic. What was a shock-and-awe feel for the prophet should no longer dazzle and delight the present man. We are at an age where we understand the dynamics of flying jets. The Gods were using even more advanced jets than man's most advanced technologically manufactured ones. As we shall find later the Gods' use of crafts is not new, for that was how they got to earth long before man was reengineered. We seem to lose sight of this particular mode of transportation mentioned in the Bible.

Interpreting Ezekiel 10:1–9:

10 Then I looked, and behold, in the firmament that was above the head of the cherubims there appeared over them, as it were, a sapphire stone with the appearance of the likeness of a throne.

2 And He spoke unto the man clothed with linen, and said, "Go in between the wheels, even under the cherub, and fill thine hand with coals of fire from between the cherubims, and scatter them over the city." And he went in in my sight.

³ Now the cherubims stood on the right side of the house when the man went in; and the cloud filled the inner court.

⁴ Then the glory of the Lord went up from the cherub and stood over the threshold of the house; and the house was filled with the cloud, and the court was full of the brightness of the Lord's glory.

⁵ And the sound of the cherubims' wings was heard even to the outer court, as the voice of the Almighty God when He speaketh.

⁶ And it came to pass that when He had commanded the man clothed with linen, saying, "Take fire from between the wheels, from between the cherubims," then he went in and stood beside the wheels.

⁷ And one cherub stretched forth his hand from between the cherubims unto the fire that was between the cherubims, and took thereof and put it into the hands of him that was clothed with linen, who took it and went out.

⁸ And there appeared in the cherubims the form of a man's hand under their wings.

⁹ And when I looked, behold, the four wheels by the cherubims, one wheel by one cherub and another wheel by another cherub; and the appearance of the wheels was as the color of a beryl stone.

The above poetic narrative is filled with varying imagery. It is thus these images that some take for granted in their varying manipulative attempts at creating an imagined story from a nonexisting narrative. They invent through the mind's creation, things not written nor intended, and the result is usually chaos.

There is a great deal of poetic material in the Bible—the Psalms, Proverbs, Ecclesiastes, some portions of the prophets, but it is not limited to the Old Testament. Now we know from reading the psalms that biblical poetry is filled with images such as: (i) shepherds, (ii) fortresses, (iii) solid rocks, (iv) stars, (v) floods, (vi) swords, (vii) darkness, (viii) light, etc. With the use of metaphors and images some interpreters erroneously think that the writer is appealing primarily to the senses. Therefore, they tend to then create their own images in their minds, thus, obliterating the meaning of the original text. Therefore, in reading and teaching the books there will be the need to unpack the significance of the images though through a generous use of the senses, feelings, and imagination, but most importantly, logic. What have we learned as modern man that the prophets did not know at their time? The answer is simply . . . a lot. In fact, the structure of many poems is built on the movement from one image to another. You will want to outline many poems according to the progression of ideas or images which move throughout the poem. Some biblical books are exhibits of poetry at their best.

Now, let us interpret the portion of Ezekiel 10:1–9 quoted above in modern, everyday language.

1. As I looked up at the heavens, I observed that in front of the helicopter was a screen shining brightly, emitting such a glow as a sapphire stone would. In front of the screen was a pilot's seat (throne).

2. Then one of the pilots, perhaps the head pilot, spoke to give directives to another pilot dressed in his space attire. The head pilot asked another pilot to check the nuclear furnace and clear any debris that might have been sucked and burned up. Clean it out.

3. When this task was performed, the helicopters were landed and stood on the south side of the temple. Combustion smoke filled the inner court of the temple.

4.   Then, the craft carrier (glory of the LORD) flew up, leaving the helicopters below and hovered over the temple. As the craft carrier hovered, smoke was all over the temple and the craft's lights shined on the temple. The brightness of the light from the craft was intense.

5.   Meanwhile, the helicopters' wings were rotating intensely and one could hear the noise like when God spoke. To speak from that height, all you need is a loudspeaker.

6.   Then the head pilot directed one of his subordinates to check the nuclear engine of the helicopter and clear out some already combusted materials.

7.   To do this, the mechanical hand of the helicopter was deployed to clean out the combustion area and the radioactive materials put in the hands of the one suited up for this kind of job.

8.   The helicopter appeared to have the form of a man's hand. That is the mechanical hand emanating from under the rotor blades-otherwise described as the wings.

9.   And as I watched, the helicopters had four wheels, one wheel by each helicopter appeared to be the color of a beryl stone-in other words, a wheel in each of the helicopters shined so bright.

Now, you can see that Prophet Ezekiel was actually describing beings with highly technological machines. He described also how they operated, even though he knew not what they were. That he chose descriptions such as "the glory of the Lord" and "full of the brightness of the LORD's glory" were appropriate since he himself is shocked and awed. How else would he have described these things? He lacked the vocabulary to describe such technologies.

It will not be surprising if some start shouting "holy cow" at the above description which is, of course, true and logical. This is not because I just proved that it is logical. With the above, you may want to get the Pentateuch and start reading afresh and see the books come alive from a different perspective and with facts. Like I have always written, I want you to believe *with facts* and not faith. Or at least understand the facts to help cement your faith.

Now, can you put your finger on how the above interpretation shatters the omnipresence myth of biblical Yahweh? There will be more on this topic in the next chapter. You may have a need for the above interpretation when you read chapter 14.

CHAPTER 11

Omnipresence Doubts

To the misinformed, the Spirit of the Lord is just that—God's Spirit. It is by this Spirit that God is everywhere. It is by this Spirit that He is omnipresent. He is present in your daily everyday activities. He is present while you are in the bathroom, while you are with your wife, while you are doing evil or doing good. He is by His attribute and power of the Spirit of the Lord everywhere. Since He is everywhere, if there was a hell, He is there too. I do not subscribe to the concept of hell personally. Let us justify all that has been said above using Psalm 139:7–12.

Where can I go from your Spirit? Or where can I flee from your presence? If I ascend into heaven, you are there; if I make my bed in hell, behold, you are there; if I take the wings of the morning and dwell in the uttermost parts of the sea, even there your hand shall lead me, and your right hand shall hold me. If I say, "Surely the darkness will hide me and the light become night around me," even the darkness will not be dark to you; the night will shine like the day, for darkness is as light to you (Psalm 139:7–12).

Does this mean that God is physically present everywhere? Of course not. But by use of a concept of the Spirit of the Lord, interpreters of the Bible gave birth to the concept of OMNIPRESENCE. They know that this is not to say that God's form is spread out so that parts of Him exist in every location. So to make it reasonable, God has to be presented as a spirit that has no physical form. Hmm, but Moses saw Him and talked to Him face to face. Moses even saw His back features. God even told us His image. God's image is that of a man. Sorry for that little diversion. According to some interpreters of the books, God is present everywhere in that everything is immediately in His presence everywhere in the universe. No one can hide from Him, and nothing escapes His notice. WOW! That wow word is lovely, especially when I am thinking very hard to understand a concept. The more I try, the more I find interpreters' misinterpretation of the book or texts that were doctored to explain a particular attribute of God. By these attributes, man created a God man wants. But read on, for we shall resolve this confusion.

Interpreters of the book quote verses such as the ones below to give credence to "Spirit of the Lord" and other concepts and attributes. Emphasis is heavily laid on the Spirit of the Lord or Spirit of God here for it is through the Spirit of the Lord that He is omnipresent.

- Though they dig into hell, from there my hand shall take them; though they climb up to heaven, from there I will bring them down; and though they hide themselves on top of Carmel, from there I will search and take them; though they hide from my sight at the bottom of the sea, from there I will command the serpent, and it shall bite them (Amos 9:2–3).

- Am I a God near at hand, says the Lord, and not a God afar off? Can anyone hide himself in secret places, so I shall not see him?... do I not fill heaven and earth? says the Lord. (Jeremiah 23:23–24)

- The eyes of the Lord are in every place, watching the evil and the good (Proverbs 15:3).

But can we truly understand the omnipresence of God? If we read the books carefully, yes, we can understand. What we are wrestling with is lack of understanding that has led to misinterpretations and confusion.

The concept of omnipresence of God has caused controversy and concern for many individuals. It will continue to do so. I say this because many people in their zest to portray the biblical Yahweh as the Ultimate Universal Creator have resorted to according Him attributes that only the Universal Creator possesses. In the midst of catastrophic events, people ask, "Where is/was God?" In frustration, some people reply, "God can't be in two places at the same time!" But by the concept of omnipresence, God can be everywhere simultaneously—that is the meaning of omnipresence—nothing escapes His attention.

Since God is eternal, spatial dimensions cannot restrict Him. God's time is infinite; therefore, God is also unrestricted with respect to space, i.e., omnipresent. You see, the more of these encomiums that are poured on this biblical God, the more the evidence shows that these encomiums are misdirected. These are the encomiums for the One Supreme Universal Creator whose name is not known.

The omnipresence of God stipulates that He cannot be contained by the largest space possible. Though God does not have spatial limitations, He does not simply exist in a kind of infinite, unending space. According to some interpreters, God is present *to* all space. There is an error, however, in thinking of God in merely spatial terms, as if He is a gigantic being like portrayed in some arts. While some will speculate that God is a Being who exists without size and dimensions in space, He, Himself, told us in no confusing terms what He looks like. Therefore, it is beyond my imagination why people continue to speculate on how God looks. God looks like a man, albeit a giant. Did I hear you question why I described him as a giant? The Bible said His sons (giants) copulated with women (Genesis 6:4). Remember, God is very strong on "a kind bringing forth same kind."

At the foundation for this omnipresence concept is, I repeat, **"The Spirit of the Lord" for according to interpreters, God is everywhere in spirit.** Are they talking about the biblical Yahweh or the Universal Creator? For to answer this question we need to research further as the answer is right there under our very nose in the book of Genesis. Genesis, first sentence after the "In the beginning . . ." opening and the description of physical earth was the description of the landing of the superintelligent Beings.

Genesis 1: 2: And the earth was without form, and void; and darkness was upon the face of the deep. *And the Spirit of God moved upon the face of the waters.* Now, what does the Spirit of God mean? The answer is in the next chapters.

You may wish to call them Elohim. You may call them Gods with a leader if you wish. Or you may choose to call them God and the angels. Any name that rocks your boat is fine. But there is no denying that superintelligent Beings we, man, have come to call God and angels, do exist. To say, therefore, that there is no "God" or "Gods" is a pointer to the pervading ignorance sowed by the misinterpretation, confusion, and fabrication of the texts of the book of Genesis and others. Now, let us reason together, but please, I beg of you, have an open mind. We must read to understand, not fabricate nonexistent events. Let us look at the meaning of *the Spirit of the Lord* for in those few words lay the truth. *The Spirit of the LORD!* But before we create a chapter to explain the Spirit of the LORD, let us first read a chapter wholly lifted from the book of the prophet Ezekiel.

CHAPTER 12

Prophet Ezekiel and the Aircrafts

The book of Prophet Ezekiel perhaps magnifies the misrepresentations and misinterpretations of the Bible. The misrepresentation is so apparent, yet people still get fooled into believing the wrong connotations of this book, and ultimately, the entire Bible. I have chosen Chapter 10 to show the confusion as they are stacked like sardines from one false interpretation to another. But first, let me reproduce below Ezekiel Chapter 10, followed by two interpretations by eminent theological interpreters. These will be followed quickly with my simple interpretation of Ezekiel Chapter 10.

Ezekiel 10
21st Century King James Version (KJ21)

10 Then I looked, and behold, in the firmament that was above the head of the cherubims there appeared over them, as it were, a sapphire stone with the appearance of the likeness of a throne.

2 And He spoke unto the man clothed with linen, and said, "Go in between the wheels, even under the cherub, and fill thine hand with coals of fire from between the cherubims, and scatter them over the city." And he went in in my sight.

³ *Now the cherubims stood on the right side of the house when the man went in; and the cloud filled the inner court.*

⁴ *Then the glory of the Lord went up from the cherub and stood over the threshold of the house; and the house was filled with the cloud, and the court was full of the brightness of the Lord's glory.*

⁵ *And the sound of the cherubims' wings was heard even to the outer court, as the voice of the Almighty God when He speaketh.*

⁶ *And it came to pass that when He had commanded the man clothed with linen, saying, "Take fire from between the wheels, from between the cherubims," then he went in and stood beside the wheels.*

⁷ *And one cherub stretched forth his hand from between the cherubims unto the fire that was between the cherubims, and took thereof and put it into the hands of him that was clothed with linen, who took it and went out.*

⁸ *And there appeared in the cherubims the form of a man's hand under their wings.*

⁹ *And when I looked, behold, the four wheels by the cherubims, one wheel by one cherub and another wheel by another cherub; and the appearance of the wheels was as the color of a beryl stone.*

¹⁰ *And as for their appearance, all four had one likeness, as if a wheel had been in the midst of a wheel.*

¹¹ *When they went, they went upon their four sides. They turned not as they went, but to the place whither the head looked they followed it; they turned not as they went.*

¹² *And their whole body, and their backs, and their hands, and their wings, and the wheels, were full of eyes round about— even the wheels that the four had.*

¹³ *As for the wheels, it was cried unto them in my hearing, "O wheel."*

¹⁴ *And every one had four faces: the first face was the face of a cherub, and the second face was the face of a man, and the third the face of a lion, and the fourth the face of an eagle.*

¹⁵ *And the cherubims were lifted up. This is the living creature that I saw by the River of Chebar.*

¹⁶ *And when the cherubims went, the wheels went alongside them; and when the cherubims lifted up their wings to mount up from the earth, the same wheels also turned not from beside them.*

¹⁷ *When they stood, these stood, and when they were lifted up, these lifted up themselves also; for the spirit of the living creature was in them.*

¹⁸ *Then the glory of the Lord departed from off the threshold of the house and stood over the cherubims.*

¹⁹ *And the cherubims lifted up their wings and mounted up from the earth in my sight. When they went out, the wheels also were beside them, and every one stood at the door of the east gate of the Lord's house; and the glory of the God of Israel was over above them.*

²⁰ *This is the living creature that I saw under the God of Israel by the River of Chebar; and I knew that they were the cherubims.*

²¹ Every one had four faces apiece, and every one four wings, and the likeness of the hands of a man was under their wings.

²² And the likeness of their faces was the same as the faces which I saw by the River of Chebar, their appearances and themselves. They went every one straight forward.

EZEKIEL 10: THE THRONE AND CHERUBIM, CHERUB AND WHEELS, LIVING CREATURE AND OTHER IMAGES. FIRST INTERPRETATION:

I have listened to and read many interpretations of the book of Ezekiel. These interpretations are either misguided or misinformed or both. They all introduce nonexistent images or misinterpret the images that the prophet was describing. Most of the interpretations allocate spiritual meaning(s) to these words.

1. The throne

2. Living creature

3. Wheels

4. Four faces

5. Cherubim and cherub

6. Jerusalem

7. Cloud, ashes, bright light, and other images . . .
   An example below is one of the interpretations. They all have one thing in common: They input spirituality where physical events happened.

"Ezekiel 10:1 Then I looked, and, behold, in the firmament that was above the head of the cherubims there appeared over them as it were a sapphire stone, as the appearance of the likeness of a throne. The prophet's vision continues; it began in Ezekiel 8:3 when he was transported by a lock of his hair to the Temple in Jerusalem. Hence, the vision was long. Chapter 10 is similar to Chapter 1. Ezekiel had this vision experience while at his house in captivity in Babylon. The ancients of Israel sat before him. In other words, he was carried away in *vision only*, for he remained where he was *physically*."

From the above and based on my explanations, one can see immediately the misinformation and misinterpretation. Ezekiel was physically pulled into the throne—the euphemism for aircraft.

Now, read more of the theologian's interpretations:

Later, after Ezekiel came out of the trance, he recorded the details of the vision. God similarly favored Moses with a vision and gave him tremendous information—all the parts of the Law, including the Tabernacle construction. In both cases, God helped their memories so that they would have perfect recall. On the firmament above the cherubim heads was God's sapphire stone throne (blue being a symbol of faithfulness and an indication that behind God's judgments are a blessing). The firmament was like a platform, and on the platform was the throne. Stated another way, the "firmament" was like frozen sky or atmosphere, and on top of the firmament was the sapphire throne. In Exodus 24:10, pertaining to the vision God gave to Moses, the "firmament" is called "a paved work." Moses and a select few went up into Mount Sinai and there saw a symbolic representation of God.

Ezekiel 10:2: And he spake unto the man clothed with linen, and said, Go in between the wheels, even under the cherub, and fill thine hand with coals of fire from between the cherubims, and scatter them over the city. And he went in in my sight. *God spoke to the man clothed in linen: "Go in between the wheels, even under the cherub [Justice], and fill thine hand with coals of fire from between the cherubims, and scatter them over the city." Ezekiel, in vision, was on the ground, looking up at the* **huge** *wheels that touched the earth. The "coals of fire" (plural) were related to* **judgment***. The man with the inkhorn, described now as being clothed in linen, had stood beside the Brazen Altar earlier (Ezekiel*

*9:2). He had put a mark on all those in the city who did not cry and sigh regarding the abominations. Now he was instructed to go **under** the throne between the wheels. There was fire both under the throne and above it—even a bright glow in the appearance of God on the throne. As narrated in Ezekiel 1:4–5, the prophet had seen a whirlwind come out of the north. In the midst of the whirlwind was a self-feeding fire. Hence the fire was extensive.*

The above is absolute nonsense. There is introduction of spirituality where no spirituality existed. There is an attempt to interpret words such as cherubims, sapphire, cherub, coals of fire as deemed fit. Ezekiel is narrating a physical happening event. Nothing spiritual. In later chapters, I will explain the physical nature of the abovementioned objects. Watchword here is *objects*—not spirituality. Oh, how man is easily fooled.

The theologian's interpretation continued:

*Why was the man clothed in linen told to go in between the wheels? What is the significance? Wheels are a symbol of progress, ages, and time sequence, and the huge wheels represent large epochs and dispensations. Therefore, God was instructing Ezekiel to go in between the ages. The Harvest, which is a little loop of time **between** the ages or, stated another way, in the overlapping of the Millennial and Gospel ages. (Ages can overlap but not the Creative Days or the worlds.) As the Gospel Age is phasing out, the Millennial Age is slowly being ushered in. The coals of fire that were to be scattered over the city (Babylon, Christendom) picture a **worldwide** message. The Ezekiel class, the feet members, are to give a **strong, burning, purgative message with a judgment feature**. Knowing that the coals of fire placed on Isaiah's lips signify a message helps to unlock the meaning of the coals here in Ezekiel (Isa. 6:6–9).*

Ezekiel 10:3: Now the cherubims stood on the right side of the house, when the man went in; and the cloud filled the inner court. Ezekiel 10:4: Then the glory of the LORD went up from the cherub, and stood over the threshold of the house; and the house was filled with the cloud, and the court was full of the brightness of the LORD'S glory.

God's glory departed from the cherubim and went over the threshold of the Temple of Solomon. In other words, the throne of God moved over the threshold, and the Temple was filled with smoke. Ezekiel Chapters 43 and 44 provide background information; in fact, Ezekiel 43:1–5 furnishes the key to understanding chapter 10. Chapters 1, 10, and 43 are connected. The Lord came in by way of the east gate. "The glory of the LORD came into the house [Temple] by the way of the gate whose prospect is toward the east . . . and, behold, the glory of the LORD filled the house" (Ezek. 43:4–5). Ezekiel went in vision into the Inner Court to see the resplendent glory where God had entered. Ezekiel 44:1–2 states that God Himself shut the Temple east gate, which represents the closing of the door forever to the high calling. God will enter into and accept His Church and formalize the acceptance. The world will be unaware of this momentous event until later. The happenings in Ezekiel pertaining to the shutting of the east gate are related to the shutting of the door in the Parable of the Wise and Foolish Virgins. In the parable, the foolish virgins knock to get in, but the door has already been shut. After the door is shut and the high calling ceases, the cherubim depart from the Temple (Ezek. 10:18–19). The east gate portrays the way of sacrifice, the way of entering in. In the final picture, it is the way of the kings of the east (Rev. 16:12).

OK. Enough already. This interpretation, like many other interpretations of the book of Ezekiel, is a guesswork sautéed with imagined imageries to arrive at a connotation that is false. And that is what is taught to a lot of religiously inclined. If you are interested in reading the whole article, a link is provided on the reference page.

The interpretation went on to introduce the church, thus:

This change of position by the Lord represents that the Church is complete and glorified, and God's acceptance is shown when the cloud fills the Temple. Likewise, upon completion of the Tabernacle and Solomon's Temple, a cloud filled the structure to show God's acceptance.

What church is the interpreter talking about here? Here again, you must have noticed how meanings are conjured up as most of the interpreters deemed necessary.

Now, read the remaining portions of the interpretation, beginning from verse 5. Your take should focus on the spiritual input of the interpretation so that when the physical interpretation is given, you would notice the big difference in the meanings.

Ezek. 10:5: And the sound of the cherubims' wings was heard even to the outer court, as the voice of the Almighty God when he speaketh. *Like a loudspeaker, the wings magnified God's voice to the Outer Court (the* **world***), saying "Peace, be still." The Lord's voice came through the wings, through the loudspeaker. In other words, God spoke with* **authority***.*

As soon as the Lord stood over the Temple, it was filled with smoke, and a tremendous luminescence shone out and filled the Inner Court. Next, God spoke powerfully so that His voice was heard in the Outer Court.

Ezek. 10:6: And it came to pass, that when he had commanded the man clothed with linen, saying, Take fire from between the wheels, from between the cherubims; then he went in, and stood beside the wheels. *Ezek. 10:7: And one cherub stretched forth his hand from between the cherubims unto the fire that was between the cherubims, and took thereof, and put it into the hands of him that was clothed with linen: who took it, and went out.*

Although the man clothed in linen went in between the wheels to get the coals of fire, the coals were actually handed to him by the **Justice** *cherub. The account goes back and forth,* **reviewing** *how the man clothed in linen got the coals of fire. Other books of the Bible (Daniel, Revelation, etc.) use this same technique of review. Usually the retracing picks up the thread at another point. In other words, the man clothed in linen went in between the wheels prior to the appearance of the glory of the Lord. This is a flashback to what happened to the man with the inkhorn. The coals of fire are a review of the work already accomplished by the six men with slaughter weapons (that is, with the* **Volumes***). The review confirms the* *interpretation of a condemning message on Babylon.* **Individual** *nominal Christians, as well as the nominal* **systems,** *are to be tried and judged.*

Chapter 1 explained that whenever the wheels were lifted up or went down, the cherubim went up or down too and vice versa. The spirit in the wheel was like the spirit in the cherub; that is, the same motivation, energy, or will was in both. Now verse 11 adds an interesting detail: When the chariot moved and the wheels went, they went "whither the head looked." The particular cherub **face of intent** *assumed the forefront position on the head stock of each cherub. Then the cherub went straight forward—with no deviation—in the direction the head looked.*

Ezek. 10:12: And their whole body, and their backs, and their hands, and their wings, and the wheels, were full of eyes round about, even the wheels that they four had.

Each entire cherub, plus its wheel and wings, was covered with "eyes," a symbol of wisdom and intelligence.

Ezek. 10:13: As for the wheels, it was cried unto them in my hearing, O wheel.

The wheels are called "whirring wheels," a term that gives the thought of **movement**—*that the ages are* **progressing.** *Especially the smaller inner wheel (verse 10) was "whirring." Since Ezekiel was getting an accelerated view of events, the little inner wheel seemed to be turning rapidly. However, both the larger and the smaller wheels were coming* **to the same terminus.** *The inner wheel was more active, but the outer wheel was moving too. God had given prophecies of the coming destruction through Ezekiel, Jeremiah, and other prophets, but nothing seemed to be happening. In regard to the end of this age, when the trouble starts to occur, events will happen* **quickly;** *an aspect of the trouble will be* **sudden.** *When the Flood came, the first long dispensation or "world" ended, but also the smaller "120-year" age ended; that is, both terminated together. At the end of the week when Noah went into the Ark, everything ended: the first 1,656-year world, the 120 years, and the 7-day week. All things came to a focal point and significant time of judgment.*

In antitype who will see the whirring wheels? The Ezekiel class, the feet members, will discern them. The smaller wheel moves fast enough to be seen plainly—action is indicated—whereas the larger wheel is seen by faith.

Q: Since Ezekiel was watching the man clothed in linen, wouldn't this indicate that the feet members will have to recognize present truth in order to take the proper stand?

A: The feet members will have to recognize present truth but not necessarily in the same manner. Although they will have to come to the same conclusion, they will come from different backgrounds. Therefore, some will get an acceleration of information that will seem amazing.

Comment: The understanding would have its seeds with the Pastor's writings, but the details of dispensational truth clarify as the light shines brighter (Prov. 4:18).

Back there Ezekiel's message was helpful and faith-strengthening to those who heard it.

Ezekiel would have been aware of Jeremiah's message and vice versa. The influence of these two prophets in different areas had a very encouraging and enlightening effect. But the different spheres of influence in their ministries are only a picture of something much more significant at the end of this dispensation.

Ezek. 10:14: And every one had four faces: the first face was the face of a cherub, and the second face was the face of a man, and the third the face of a lion, and the fourth the face of an eagle.

Each cherub had four faces. The "face of a cherub" should be the "face of an ox," as in the vision by the river Chebar in chapter 1. The four faces were of an ox, a man, a lion, and an eagle. Thus the Bible corrects itself. This error was permitted to creep into the text to stumble those who do not look for internal evidence. Revelation 4:7 also shows the face to be that of a calf or an ox.

Ezek. 10:15: And the cherubims were lifted up. This is the living creature that I saw by the river of Chebar.

Ezek. 10:16: And when the cherubims went, the wheels went by them: and when the cherubims lifted up their wings to mount up from the earth, the same wheels also turned not from beside them.

Ezek. 10:17: When they stood, these stood; and when they were lifted up, these lifted up themselves also: for the spirit of the living creature was in them.

*Verses 16 and 17 emphasize the **oneness** of the wheels and the cherubim. They acted alike; the **same spirit** was in both. The character of the wheels is being emphasized in relation to the cherubim. Since the wheels represent ages, the wheels-cherubim relationship shows that God moves according to a plan. Stated another way, God's attributes operate in harmony with a predetermined plan.*

The action of the wheels so impressed Ezekiel that he realized the same spirit was in both the cherubim and the wheels. Each wheel and each cherub had a spirit, and their spirits acted in unison. They moved together because the same spirit motivated both.

Ezek. 10:18: Then the glory of the LORD departed from off the threshold of the house, and stood over the cherubims.

Ezek. 10:19: And the cherubims lifted up their wings, and mounted up from the earth in my sight: when they went out, the wheels also were beside them, and every one stood at the door of the east gate of the LORD'S house; and the glory of the God of Israel was over them above.

Now the posture of Jehovah changed. The glory of the Lord, which was seated on or over the Temple, returned to its normal position on the platform above the cherubim. In other words, the glory of God first departed off the cherubim platform, then went to sit on the Temple, and now returned to the platform.

*This scene took place in the rather spacious Inner Court. The east gate was the way into the Inner Court (as were the gates on the north and south sides). Here, in regard to **Solomon's** Temple, God temporarily got* *out of the chariot, sat on the Temple, and then went back to the chariot; next the chariot moved to the east gate and paused there. In regard to* **Ezekiel's** *Temple of the future, the glory of the Lord will enter by way of the east gate, and the east gate will be shut (Ezekiel 43:1–4; 44:1). The Temple will then symbolically be God's residence.*

Ezekiel 10:20: This is the living creature that I saw under the God of Israel by the river of Chebar; and I knew that they were the cherubims.

Ezekiel 10:21: Every one had four faces apiece, and every one four wings; and the likeness of the hands of a man was under their wings.

Ezekiel 10:22: And the likeness of their faces was the same faces which I saw by the river of Chebar, their appearances and themselves: they went every one straight forward.

Every cherub (with its wheel) went "straight forward" when in motion. First, the heads swiveled to the appropriate attribute for the action about to take place, and then the cherubim moved in that direction.

"The likeness of their faces was the same faces which I saw by the river of Chebar." The discrepancy in the faces in verse 14 is corrected here by the referral back to the vision in chapter 1. Obviously, all four **cherubim** *had* **cherub** *faces, so the "face of a cherub" should be the "face of an ox."*

Verses 15, 20, and 22 all state that these are the same cherubim that were by the river Chebar in chapter 1. Because the vision is important in **all** *of its detail, many of the facets are repeated (wings, wheels, faces, etc.). This is a vision of* **Almighty** *God's character, movement, and operation . . .*

. . . What is the significance of the statement "And the posts of the door moved at the voice of him that cried, and the house was filled with smoke"? When Isaiah saw the vibration and shaking of the posts, he was frightened, saying in verse 5, "Woe is me! for I am undone; because I am a man of unclean lips." The destruction of the spiritual professed Church or Temple of the Lord and the indwelling of the Spirit of the true Temple of the Lord are somewhat coincidental. The professed nominal Church of this age will be replaced by the true Temple. The smoke that fills the Temple is

*usually associated with the completion of the Church and the dedication of the Temple or Tabernacle. Thus it is a **holy** smoke. The moving posts suggest removal and yet institution. Babylon's fall will be an evidence that the Church is complete. As Babylon, the professed Temple of this age, is removed, the true Church will be instituted. The fact that no man could enter Solomon's Temple until the smoke of God's acceptance subsided means that the service of the priesthood on behalf of the **world** will not start until the true Church is complete and glorified (1 Kings 8:10–11).*

The true Church will be gone by the middle of Babylon's rise to power or hour of power. The half hour of silence that follows will be terminated by Babylon's fall. During that half hour—or at least by the end of the half hour of silence when Babylon falls—the Great Company will realize the Church is gone.

*In chapter 1, Ezekiel saw judgment coming upon **fleshly** Israel. Now, in chapter 10, the prophet saw judgment coming on **spiritual** Israel.*

Watch the summary drawn for Ezekiel 1 and 10. There was absolutely nothing flesh or spiritual in them. Ezekiel, here, just narrated what he was observing physically. We shall read this author's explanation in subsequent chapters.

Meanwhile, let us look at another interpretation of the same Ezekiel chapters and verses in the next chapter.

CHAPTER 13

A Different Interpretation of Ezekiel 10.

It is very important here to recognize that in most of these theological interpretations of Ezekiel, spirituality is the focus. Physicality was never considered. Therein lies the problem.

Spirituality has become a much-used and abused word in the interpretation of biblical narratives yesterday and even today. The intent has always been to create an aura of a spiritual connotation. In our newfound escape/garb of spirituality, we forget that we are multidimensional beings, made up of body, mind, intellect, and spirit. Each component has a very well-defined role and such a role is as important as any in the scheme of things, large or small. The physical has been dumped in a trash can of ignorance. What is physical? Physical is something that consumes three dimensions of space and volume. There is also the mental, which involves thoughts, ideas, and imagination. By spiritual—something between the two (physical and mental) becomes a blur. The blur is simply the perception of one's own ignorance. And because man was more ignorant in the past, anything that cannot be explained became shock and awe. It became spirituality where physicality and only physicality obtained. When it comes to biblical explanations, even our best educated become ignorant, not because they are not smart, but because they cannot imagine certain events happening at such a time where such knowledge was expected not to exist. It was supposed to be beyond comprehension. Below is another interpretation of Ezekiel 10 by an academic theologian.

COFFMAN'S COMMENTARIES ON EZEKIEL 10:

In verse 1, Coffman infers the burning of Jerusalem and withdrawal of God's presence. He explains further:

Here we have a continuation of the major theme of Ezekiel 8–11, which particularly deals with the final departure of the presence of God from the apostate capitol of the Once Chosen people. Ezekiel 10:1–8 prophesy the burning of Jerusalem; and Ezekiel 9:9–22 show preparations for the withdrawal of God's presence, his final departure being revealed in the next chapter.

Ezekiel 10:1–4

Then I looked, and, behold, in the firmament that was over the head of the cherubim there appeared above them as it were a sapphire stone, as the appearance of the likeness of a throne. And he spake unto the man clothed in linen, and said, Go in between the whirling wheels, even under the cherub, and fill both thy hands with coals of fire from between the cherubim, and scatter them over the city. And he went in in my sight. Now the cherubim stood on the right side of the house, when the man went in; and the cloud filled the inner court. And the glory of Jehovah mounted up from the cherub, and stood over the threshold of the house; and the house was filled with the cloud, and the court was full of the brightness of Jehovah's glory.

"Coals of fire . . . scatter them over the city . . ." (Ezekiel 10:2). This sentence of Jerusalem's destruction took place in the Temple itself, "Thus making it manifest that the judgment is in vindication of the affronted holiness of God, caused by the sins of Israel against his covenant."[1]

"And he spake . . ." (Ezekiel 10:2). The speaker here is the person enthroned, namely, God.

The fire spoken of in this passage is far different from the fire of the altar. "That fire spoke of God's grace (Leviticus 6:1–13); here it speaks of the destruction of the wicked."[2]

Pearson noted that in Ezekiel 10:2 a singular noun is used to describe the whole complex of whirling wheels, etc., supporting the sapphire throne. [3] This indicates that the entire apparatus had the utility of standing as a representation of the presence and glory of the Almighty.

"The glory of Jehovah mounted up from the cherub . . ." . Cook used the past perfect tense here. "'The glory of the Lord had gone up from the cherub to the threshold of the house,' to describe what had happened before the man went in (v. 3)."[4] This description runs through verse 6.

Verse 5

"And the sound of the wings of the cherubim was heard even to the outer court, as the voice of God Almighty when he speaketh. And it came to pass when he commanded the man clothed in linen, saying, Take fire from between the whirling wheels, from between the cherubim, that he went in and stood beside a wheel. And the cherub stretched forth his hand from between the cherubim unto the fire that was between the cherubim, and took fire thereof, and put it into the hands of him that was clothed in linen, who took it and went out. And there appeared in the cherubim the form of a man's hand under their wings."

"The sound of the wings . . ." (Ezekiel 10:5). This great sound is variously described as very loud, as the voice of the Almighty, as of a "rushing mighty wind," etc. Significantly, in the New Testament on the Day of Pentecost, when God's glory was manifested by the appearance of the Holy Spirit upon the holy apostles, that event also was marked by forked flames as of fire and the "sound of a rushing mighty wind" (Acts 2:2).

According to Coffman, *"The great significance of this chapter is that the very manifestation of God's glory which had appeared to Ezekiel in Babylon at the Chebar river (canal) is here seen in the process of deserting the Temple in Jerusalem, strongly indicating that God's concern in the future from the destruction of Jerusalem would rest with the exiles in Babylon and not with any stragglers left in Jerusalem.*

"Who took it and went out . . ." (Ezekiel 10:7). "Nothing is said here of the actual scattering of fire over the city." [5] The same author explained that no account of his actually doing so is necessary, "Because, it often happens in Scripture that a prophet mentions a command without describing the actual execution of it." [6] It must always be assumed, if not stated to the contrary, that God's commandments were executed exactly as commanded.

"The form of a man's hand . . ." (Ezekiel 10:8). "The appearance of this indicates that human agencies would be utilized in the execution of God's judgment upon Israel." [7] It would never have been necessary for the Angel of Jehovah himself, the one clad in linen, to scatter coals of fire in any personal sense over Jerusalem. As Beasley-Murray stated it, "This vision prophesies the fires that destroyed Jerusalem in 587 B.C. (2 Kings 25:9), by the armies of the Chaldeans." [8] In a very similar way, the fires that again destroyed Jerusalem in 70 A.D. were prophetically identified by Jesus Christ himself as "God's armies" (Matthew 22:7).

Such passages as these indicate that God is the prime agent in all human history, whatever human agencies may be employed from time to time in the achievement of God's eternal purpose.

"The most significant thing here is the identity of the Destroyer as God." [9] "The maneuvering of God's Glory in this chapter shows that God, whom men thought to be inseparably bound to his sanctuary and to his city of Jerusalem, is about to destroy both of them and to abandon their ruins." [10]

Verse 9

"And I looked, and behold, four wheels beside the cherubim, one wheel beside one cherub, and another wheel beside another cherub; and the appearance of the whole was like a beryl stone. And as for their appearance, they four had one likeness, as if a wheel had been within a

wheel. When they went, they went in their four directions: they turned not as they went, but to the place whither the head looked they followed it; they turned not as they went. And their whole body, and their backs, and their hands, and the wings, and the wheels, were full of eyes round about, even the wheels that they four had. As for the wheels, they were called in my hearing the whirling wheels. And every one had four faces: the first face was the face of the cherub, and the second was that of a man, and the third the face of a lion, and the fourth the face of an eagle."

COFFMAN EXPLAINED SOME MORE, THUS:

Ezekiel 10:9–12 is nearly identical with Ezekiel 1:15–18; and this writer cannot visualize any consistent apparatus that fits the vision. Wheels that are whirling, but do not turn as they go, and that go in four directions somehow fail to form any clear picture. The complex, complicated vision is here changed in the particular of so many eyes so widely distributed, and "the face of the cherub," is apparently substituted for the "face of an ox" in Ezekiel 1. Perhaps we are not supposed to be able thoroughly to understand it.

If the vision should have been poised to move in any other direction, the man, the lion, or the eagle would have been the "face of the cherub," depending on the direction indicated, whether north, west, or south. It was the eastward projection here that made the "ox face" the "face of the cherub."

The actions of the great Vision in this second appearance of it to Ezekiel, "Enable us here to witness the beginning of the gradual withdrawal and departure of the glory of the Lord from the city. God was not leaving it permanently; some day he would return." [13]

Yes, this was true; (see Ezekiel 43); but only in a typical sense. God's glory would never again dwell in "a temple made with hands." God's glory would indeed dwell with Israel forever; but it would be within the holy temple, namely, the Church, the New Israel of God, and not in any sense whatever with the old racial Israel that so long had denied and rebelled against God Himself. That return of God's glory to the "temple of God" occurred on the Day of Pentecost, the birthday of God's church.

Where was God's glory, or the manifestation of his Presence, located during that time between the destruction of Jerusalem until the Day of Pentecost? Its appearance in Babylon in Ezekiel 1 indicates very strongly that God's presence was with the "righteous remnant," with those "Israelites indeed," who waited for the kingdom of God (John 1:47). There does not appear to have been a very large number of those "true Israelites." The apostles of Christ, Nathaniel, Elizabeth and Zecharias, Mary and Joseph, some of the brothers of Jesus, Zacchaeus, Simeon, Anna and others were some whom we can identify.

Verse 15

"And the cherubim mounted up: this is the living creature that I saw by the river Chebar. And when the cherubim went, the wheels went beside them; and when the cherubim lifted up their wings to mount up from the earth, the wheels also turned not from beside them. When they stood, these stood, and when they mounted up, these mounted up with them: for the spirit of the living creature was in them. And the glory of Jehovah went forth from over the threshold of the house, and stood over the cherubim. And the cherubim lifted up their wings, and mounted up from the earth in my sight when they went forth: and they stood at the door of the east gate of Jehovah's house; and the glory of the God of Israel was over them above."

THE DEPARTURE OF GOD'S GLORY

"Cherubim . . . this is the living creature . . ." (Ezekiel 10:15). Note how the cherubim (plural), along with all of the other details of the vision, nevertheless refer only to One, namely, the enthroned One, who is God.

"The living creature that I saw by the river Chebar . . ." (Ezekiel 10:15). "It was a matter of importance that the identities of these two theophanies should have been established, in order to show their real *meaning." [15] Bluntly stated, those appearances meant simply that God's glorious presence was forsaking the old racial Israel, and forever afterward concentrating upon the "righteous remnant," at that time identified with the captives in Babylon.*

Only when we come to Ezekiel 10:15, here, does Ezekiel identify the "living creatures" of Ezekiel 1:5ff as "cherubim." [16] It is not surely known exactly why this was not made known earlier. See the article at end of this chapter regarding the creatures called "cherubim."

"The cherubim lifted up from the earth . . ." (Ezekiel 10:18). "From that hour, the temple would be what Shiloh had been, a God-deserted place."

As for the notion that the second temple received the same honor as the first as the resting place of the Glory and the Spirit of God, Jesus Christ took care of that falsehood forever when he denominated the temple as "a den of thieves and robbers," which it most assuredly was. Furthermore, the sons of Satan who had charge of that Second Temple were the principal agents in the contrived execution of the Son of God.

In Ezekiel 10:18, "The glory of Jehovah now moves from the threshold of the temple and stands upon the Cherubim, ready to leave." [18] Indeed, God's presence had forsaken the temple, but it would not depart from the area until the event recorded in the next chapter (Ezekiel 11:22–23). The episode recorded in Ezekiel 11:1–21 has the effect of delaying the account of the final departure.

The departure of God's glory was the departure of the aircraft. That, simply, was what it meant then and means today. That was physical. There was nothing spiritual in the narration then, and nothing spiritual in it today.

CHAPTER 14

The Simple Interpretation of Ezekiel Chapter 10

Do you recall the interpretation rendered in chapter 10 of this book using today's vocabulary? It will enhance your understanding of this chapter.

Before we dive in, let us define and understand a few choice words taken from the book *God Is Not Enough, Messiah Needed,* from pages 32 and 33.'

1.

    a.   Cherubim, according to *Encyclopedia Mythica*: are winged creatures that support the throne of God, or act as guardian spirits. They appear in the Bible (the book of Ezekiel) as bearing the throne and chariot of God.

    b.   Cherubim, according to *Bible Encyclopedia*: In the book of Enoch, cherubim, seraphim, and ophannim (wheels), and all the angels of power constitute the "host of God," the guardians of His throne . . .

    c.   Cherubim, according to *Catholic Encyclopedia*: Angelic beings or symbolic representations thereof, mentioned frequently in the Old Testament and once in the New Testament.

2.   Below is a description that differs totally from the above dictionary connotations.

Let us list a few keys to further help in unlocking these narrations, thus, helping us to see what Ezekiel saw.

    a.   Cherubim = the whole craft, but these are like helicopters

    b.   Sapphire = seat

    c.   Cloud = steam/smoke

    d.   Spirit of the living creatures = the engines/controls

    e.   The glory of the Lord = the bigger craft into which the cherubim are housed

    f.   Four faces = something like glass windows specially but differently designed

g.   Wings = think of helicopter wings/rotor blades

h.   Hands = mechanical hand for gripping

i.   Lord of spirits = the pilot

For further clarification:

j.   The throne of God = is the inside of the biggest craft (Pilot's seat)

k.   Heavens = is the atmosphere where birds and planes fly

l.   Pillar of fire = combustible materials emanating from the crafts in the atmosphere

m.   And the Lord went before them = the Lord, here, is a combination of the pilot inside the craft

The craft is named "the Spirit of the Lord."

The way and manner the phrase "the Spirit of the Lord" was used in many parts of the Bible is very problematic and indeed very confusing. In almost all instances, one could be fooled into thinking and accepting a meaning on the lines of some invisible possessive spirit that takes control of a seer or any individual. It has also been used in such a way as God possessing Saul and a whole lot of other prophets. For example, Isaiah 61:1, King James Bible:

The Spirit of the Lord GOD is upon me; because the LORD hath anointed me to preach good tidings unto the meek; he hath sent me to bind up the brokenhearted, to proclaim liberty to the captives, and the opening of the prison to them that are bound . . .

In another example, 1 Samuel 16:14, King James Bible:

But the Spirit of the LORD departed from Saul, and an evil spirit from the LORD troubled him.

One can easily see and understand the context the phrase "the Spirit of the LORD" was used here. Here it possesses the individual.

Let us compare:

In Ezekiel 37:1, King James Bible:

The hand of the LORD was upon me, and carried me out in the spirit of the LORD, and set me down in the midst of the valley which was full of bones,

In Acts 8:39, King James Bible:

And when they were come up out of the water, the Spirit of the Lord caught away Philip, that the eunuch saw him no more: and he went on his way rejoicing.

Both quotations above can be easily interpreted and visualized using the keys provided earlier. So in Ezekiel 37:1, it means that the mechanical hand of the aircraft grabbed me and carried me out of the aircraft and set me down in the midst of the valley . . . He simply was helped to disembark from an aircraft.

Acts 8:39 . . . Simply means that the aircraft whisked Philip away to another destination. There is nothing spiritual in these incidents. It is a narration of exactly how the event happened. You can see for yourself that the narrators narrated exactly what took place.

The confusion, misinterpretations, and fabrications in the texts could be avoided if one logically thinks through the context. Placing the phrase "the Spirit of the Lord" under a microscope of logic would simply diagnose in what context it was used. There would be no need to infer other inventions of imagery to further make murky of an already confusing text.

Just so we understand this context (the Spirit of the LORD as a flying aircraft) clearly, let us read two chapters from the book of Ezekiel. A detailed explanation is available in the book *God Is Not Enough* . . . Let us read from Ezekiel 1 and 10. First, chapter 1, and then Ezekiel 10 (From KJV online).

1 Now it came to pass in the thirtieth year, in the fourth month, in the fifth day of the month, as I was among the captives by the river of Chebar, that the heavens were opened, and I saw visions of God.

² In the fifth day of the month, which was the fifth year of king Jehoiachin's captivity,

³ The word of the Lord came expressly unto Ezekiel the priest, the son of Buzi, in the land of the Chaldeans by the river Chebar; and the hand of the Lord was there upon him.

⁴ And I looked, and, behold, a whirlwind came out of the north, a great cloud, and a fire infolding itself, and a brightness was about it, and out of the midst thereof as the colour of amber, out of the midst of the fire.

⁵ Also out of the midst thereof came the likeness of four living creatures. And this was their appearance; they had the likeness of a man.

⁶ And every one had four faces, and every one had four wings.

⁷ And their feet were straight feet; and the sole of their feet was like the sole of a calf's foot: and they sparkled like the colour of burnished brass.

⁸ And they had the hands of a man under their wings on their four sides; and they four had their faces and their wings.

⁹ Their wings were joined one to another; they turned not when they went; they went every one straight forward.

¹⁰ As for the likeness of their faces, they four had the face of a man, and the face of a lion, on the right side: and they four had the face of an ox on the left side; they four also had the face of an eagle.

¹¹ Thus were their faces: and their wings were stretched upward; two wings of every one were joined one to another, and two covered their bodies.

[12] And they went every one straight forward: whither the spirit was to go, they went; and they turned not when they went.

[13] As for the likeness of the living creatures, their appearance was like burning coals of fire, and like the appearance of lamps: it went up and down among the living creatures; and the fire was bright, and out of the fire went forth lightning.

[14] And the living creatures ran and returned as the appearance of a flash of lightning.

[15] Now as I beheld the living creatures, behold one wheel upon the earth by the living creatures, with his four faces.

[16] The appearance of the wheels and their work was like unto the colour of a beryl: and they four had one likeness: and their appearance and their work was as it were a wheel in the middle of a wheel.

[17] When they went, they went upon their four sides: and they turned not when they went.

[18] As for their rings, they were so high that they were dreadful; and their rings were full of eyes round about them four.

[19] And when the living creatures went, the wheels went by them: and when the living creatures were lifted up from the earth, the wheels were lifted up.

[20] Whithersoever the spirit was to go, they went, thither was their spirit to go; and the wheels were lifted up over against them: for the spirit of the living creature was in the wheels.

[21] When those went, these went; and when those stood, these stood; and when those were lifted up from the earth, the wheels were

lifted up over against them: for the spirit of the living creature was in the wheels.

22 And the likeness of the firmament upon the heads of the living creature was as the colour of the terrible crystal, stretched forth over their heads above.

23 And under the firmament were their wings straight, the one toward the other: every one had two, which covered on this side, and every one had two, which covered on that side, their bodies.

24 And when they went, I heard the noise of their wings, like the noise of great waters, as the voice of the Almighty, the voice of speech, as the noise of an host: when they stood, they let down their wings.

25 And there was a voice from the firmament that was over their heads, when they stood, and had let down their wings.

26 And above the firmament that was over their heads was the likeness of a throne, as the appearance of a sapphire stone: and upon the likeness of the throne was the likeness as the appearance of a man above upon it.

27 And I saw as the colour of amber, as the appearance of fire round about within it, from the appearance of his loins even upward, and from the appearance of his loins even downward, I saw as it were the appearance of fire, and it had brightness round about.

28 As the appearance of the bow that is in the cloud in the day of rain, so was the appearance of the brightness round about. This was the appearance of the likeness of the glory of the Lord. And when I saw it, I fell upon my face, and I heard a voice of one that spake.

Ezekiel 10 (KJV)

10 Then I looked, and, behold, in the firmament that was above the head of the cherubims there appeared over them as it were a sapphire stone, as the appearance of the likeness of a throne.

² And he spake unto the man clothed with linen, and said, Go in between the wheels, even under the cherub, and fill thine hand with coals of fire from between the cherubims, and scatter them over the city. And he went in in my sight.

³ Now the cherubims stood on the right side of the house, when the man went in; and the cloud filled the inner court.

⁴ Then the glory of the Lord went up from the cherub, and stood over the threshold of the house; and the house was filled with the cloud, and the court was full of the brightness of the Lord's glory.

⁵ And the sound of the cherubims' wings was heard even to the outer court, as the voice of the Almighty God when he speaketh.

⁶ And it came to pass, that when he had commanded the man clothed with linen, saying, Take fire from between the wheels, from between the cherubims; then he went in, and stood beside the wheels.

⁷ And one cherub stretched forth his hand from between the cherubims unto the fire that was between the cherubims, and took thereof, and put it into the hands of him that was clothed with linen: who took it, and went out.

⁸ And there appeared in the cherubims the form of a man's hand under their wings.

⁹ And when I looked, behold the four wheels by the cherubims, one wheel by one cherub, and another wheel by another cherub: and the appearance of the wheels was as the colour of a beryl stone.

¹⁰ And as for their appearances, they four had one likeness, as if a wheel had been in the midst of a wheel.

¹¹ When they went, they went upon their four sides; they turned not as they went, but to the place whither the head looked they followed it; they turned not as they went.

¹² And their whole body, and their backs, and their hands, and their wings, and the wheels, were full of eyes round about, even the wheels that they four had.

¹³ As for the wheels, it was cried unto them in my hearing, O wheel.

¹⁴ And every one had four faces: the first face was the face of a cherub, and the second face was the face of a man, and the third the face of a lion, and the fourth the face of an eagle.

¹⁵ And the cherubims were lifted up. This is the living creature that I saw by the river of Chebar.

¹⁶ And when the cherubims went, the wheels went by them: and when the cherubims lifted up their wings to mount up from the earth, the same wheels also turned not from beside them.

¹⁷ When they stood, these stood; and when they were lifted up, these lifted up themselves also: for the spirit of the living creature was in them.

¹⁸ Then the glory of the Lord departed from off the threshold of the house, and stood over the cherubims.

¹⁹ And the cherubims lifted up their wings, and mounted up from the earth in my sight: when they went out, the wheels also were beside them, and every one stood at the door of the east gate of the Lord's house; and the glory of the God of Israel was over them above.

²⁰ This is the living creature that I saw under the God of Israel by the river of Chebar; and I knew that they were the cherubims.

²¹ Every one had four faces apiece, and every one four wings; and the likeness of the hands of a man was under their wings.

²² And the likeness of their faces was the same faces which I saw by the river of Chebar, their appearances and themselves: they went every one straight forward.

The above was brought in so that you are well prepared for the next chapter. You have now been introduced to how the Gods traveled and their type of transportation. Now, if that was how the Gods traveled, can you honestly use the word *omnipresence* with a straight face?

CHAPTER 15

Omnipresence of God and His Reach

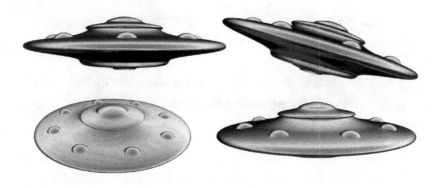

In the book, *God Is Not Enough, Messiah Needed,* I explained that the Gods have crafts—aircrafts. I explained using the book of Ezekiel as evidence and as a guide. It might be repetitious but repeat we must to further explain so as to place the confused into that group of logical thinking minds. I will therefore reproduce parts of that chapter here: In the concluding part of chapter four in the book *God Is Not Enough, Messiah Needed,* I wrote, "Other Bible chapters and verses to familiarize you with and to shed light on interpretation of the already available information are listed below. In these chapters and verses, you will see how they logically fit the interpretation of these biblical crafts. The most interesting part for me is that these quotes are from the Bible. It also goes to show that one can rely on the prophets in the Bible. They saw what they saw and wrote about the events to the best their imagination and descriptive abilities would allow. Naming these crafts "biblical crafts" as opposed to any other names in this day and age is befitting.

Let us list a few keys to further help in unlocking these narrations:

n. Cherubim = the whole craft, but these are like helicopters

o. Sapphire = seat

p. Cloud = steam/smoke

q. Spirit of the living creatures = the engines/controls

r. The glory of the Lord = the bigger craft into which the cherubim are housed

s. Four faces = something like glass windows specially but differently designed

t. Wings = think of helicopter wings/rotor blades

u. Hands = mechanical hand for gripping

v. Lord of spirits = the pilot

For further clarification:

w. The throne of God = is the inside of the biggest craft

x. Heavens = is the atmosphere where birds and planes fly

y. Pillar of fire = combustible materials emanating from the crafts in the atmosphere

z. And the Lord went before them = the Lord, here, is a combination of the pilot inside the craft"

If you have now grasped the above description of flying crafts, the simple logical question to ponder on is - If the God Ezekiel was receiving information from was omnipresent, why does He need a flying machine to go to north, south, east, and west? Did that God tell us that He is omnipresent or did man create this attribute to reverence this God? Did the interpreters of the books create the magic of omnipresence to give this God an aura of spirituality beyond human comprehension?

When we read with an open mind, the Bible is full of information that would amaze you if you understand it. The Bible has indeed told us how these incredibly powerful beings came to earth. The Bible did not hide it. It explained how God came here and what he observed and how they immediately went to work to claim the planet Earth.

According to Genesis, it was waters, waters, and more waters everywhere on planet Earth. He separated the waters for when they came the whole earth was covered with water.

Also according to Enuma Elish, the Sumerian chronology, the earth was all water. So when the beings first came here, and it was full of waters, where then did they land? Put on your seat belt for here it comes! *They did not land for there was no land.* No one is making this up. It is all there in the Bible, but it has always been misinterpreted. So, let us go to the videotape of the Bible. Let us look at various versions of the Bible to see how the words were used in Genesis 1:1–2.

Genesis 1:1–2, KJV online:

1 In the beginning God created the heaven and the earth.

[2] And the earth was without form and void, and darkness was upon the face of the deep. ***And the Spirit of God* moved upon the face of the waters.**

Genesis 1:1–2 KJV:

1 In the beginning God created the heavens and the earth

² The earth was without form, and void; and darkness was on the face of the deep. **And *the Spirit of God was hovering* over the face of the waters.**

Genesis 1:1–2 (NIV):

1 In the beginning God created the heavens and the earth.

² Now the earth was formless and empty, darkness was over the surface of the deep, **and *the Spirit of God was hovering* over the waters.**

Genesis 1:1–2 (1611 Bible, online):

1 In the beginning God created the Heaven, and the Earth.

² And the earth was without forme, and voyd, and darkenesse was vpon the face of the deepe: and the Spirit of God mooued vpon the face of the waters.

You may be asking at this moment, "Where are we going with the above?" Be patient. Do you still remember the craft named "Spirit of the Lord" in the prior chapter? Do you also see "Spirit of the Lord" hovering on the waters in the above Genesis 1 verse 2?

When it comes to being an aircraft, look for the words that have anything to do with movement—"move" and/or "hovering." So, if God traveled to earth in His "the spirit of the LORD" aircraft, does that answer the puzzle of omnipresence? Over to you to answer that. Is this enough to clear this confusion for you? As for me, I "believe" that this God exists even more than before through evidence, not by faith. It sure was not a figment of the prophets' imagination. He is real. However, the question you must ask yourself is: "Who are these intelligent beings, and who is their leader?" Do not forget that this universe has existed for approximately 9 billion years before the earth came into existence. And by the way, it cannot be ruled out that these beings had the technology to cause the earth to collide with another planet forming Earth and having a resultant remnant of the moon. Science supports that scenario too. Do you think the universe was devoid of life for those 9 billion years before Earth came into existence?

CHAPTER 16

Immutability Doubts

This will not be first time I talk about an immutable God in my books. Immutability on its own creates a meaning that causes confusion. This is so because interpreters, while they try as much as they could to extol the virtues of a God in such manner, employing attributes such as immutability, evidence points to the contrary. Sometimes, it just seems like folks are in competition to see who wins or whose interpretation is right, rather than what is right. It is a competition of "my God is bigger than yours." It is a competition of whose interpretation is more attuned to a spin rather than what the prophets intended. They seem to turn the texts into a talking point or framework to spin a simple narrative. It is a sorry state of spins.

The spinners say that immutability means unchangeable. They say it is the divine attribute of unchangeableness. In Exodus 3:14, they quote where a Being said, "I AM that I AM," signifying His eternal sameness and His sovereignty. They say He cannot change His moral character, His love, His omniscience, omnipresence, omnipotence; for He is "From everlasting to everlasting" (Psalm 90:2). It is here one begins to get confused.

All the readers and believers of the various religious books do not seem to agree on immutability as we shall see later.

Immutability does not mean that God does not vary. It does not mean that He is unchangeable. Without quoting any evidence, as a reader of the

Bible, or even just reading this work, you would notice that the God of the Old Testament is very different from the God Jesus preached or purported to symbolize. The God of the Old Testament was a God of war, killing, maiming, and angry, a do-it-my-way-or-the-highway God. Whereas, He is God of war in Old Testament, in the New Testament, He is God of LOVE. That is a very big change, don't you think?

The book teaches that God's attitude toward a person is changed when that person becomes a believer through Christ. For example, the enmity between God and man is removed (Rom. 5:10). Now, what about those who were not opportune to believe through Christ? Do you notice a modification here and, thus, a variance here?

King James Version (KJV):

6 For when we were yet without strength, in due time Christ died for the ungodly.

7 For scarcely for a righteous man will one die: yet peradventure for a good man some would even dare to die.

8 But God commendeth his love toward us, in that, while we were yet sinners, Christ died for us.

9 Much more then, being now justified by his blood, we shall be saved from wrath through him.

10 *For if, when we were enemies, we were reconciled to God by the death of his Son, much more, being reconciled, we shall be saved by his life.*

11 And not only so, but we also joy in God through our Lord Jesus Christ, by whom we have now received the atonement.

Whereas God's perfection makes it never necessary for Him to change, the God of Israel changes in His moral and other attributes. This is demonstrated by the fact that He evolved from a God of war into a God of love in the New Testament.

So far, some religions have professed their belief in a God who is God alone (Isa. 44:8), self-existent (Isa. 43:10, 48:12), transcendent (Num. 23:19; Ps. 50:21), immutable (Ps. 102:27; Isa. 46:10; Mal. 3:6), eternal (Ps. 90:2, 93:2), omnipresent (1 Kings 8:27; Prov. 15:3; Isa. 66:1; Jer. 23:23–24), and incorporeal (John 4:24; Col. 1:15; 1 Tim. 1:17). He is also a God who dwells in the believer (Eph. 3:17, 4:6; Rom. 8:9) and is omnipotent (Job 42:2; Ps. 115:3; Matt. 19:26).

So far, I have tried to explain that these attributes are being used in a bad way because proof upon proof show them to be false when applied to the biblical God. These attributes are some of the reasons people fall from faith for where knowledge ends, religion as faith is introduced.

Before we go any further, let us take from the work in my book *Why Was Man Created?* Page 117–120.

No sooner did He finish creating Adam and placing him in the Garden of Eden there came along a talking serpent that spoke and outwitted him by deceiving man—God's creation. God's divine plan and design are falling apart from the get-go. Applying the word "outwit" is describing it somberly. What really happened is a coup among the gods. The behavior of God in the Garden of Eden was very telling and will remain peculiar. The Elohim in charge of the Garden of Eden was so dictatorial and very stubborn. Where is the logic in creating a tree of knowledge and He refused man to part take of it? This singular act goes to make logic of Enki's demand that man be made "smart" . . . Meanwhile, the divine plan took another setback when the second generation turned out to be a murderer, Cain, who then kills Abel.

With time, the divine plan suffered yet another big blow as God got angry with man. Man was not following God's divine plan. Some angels outwitted God again and messed God's plans by sleeping with God's man creations. *God regrets His actions in creating man. Why was God blaming fallible man? Man should not have been punished. He should have punished the angels who messed with His divine plan. Maybe, that was not logical to God.*

In Genesis 6:7, we read, So the LORD said, "I will wipe from the face of the earth the human race I have created—and with them the animals, the birds and the creatures that move along the ground—for I regret that I have made them."

He decided to flood the Earth and start all over. Allegedly, He chose and saved Noah and his family as the most righteous people at that time while thinking that Noah & Family would populate the Earth with righteous offspring.

But soon, those sinners in Sodom and Gomorrah proved him wrong and God was angry again and He punished the cities of Sodom and Gomorrah, this time with nuclear weapons.

He introduced a covenant and offered Abraham a bargain in which He, God, would choose Abraham's offspring as His chosen people. Things went well with Abraham's offspring for some time. He, God, was hitherto with Isaac and Jacob when a great famine that forced Jacob and his children to migrate to Egypt. They languished in Egypt for hundreds of years as slaves.

Then He realized that His people must not continue as slaves, so He chose Moses to take the Israelites to a "new" land. That journey took more time than usual.

When the people complained, God made them wander in the desert for 40 years until a new generation was of age. Moses too did not set foot in the new land.

After Moses, Joshua, under the direction of God, went ahead to murder and pillage the occupants of the "new" land. Soon, the chosen people demanded a new leader. God has been leading through judges/ priests. The people wanted a king.

Saul took over as the first king. Soon, God got angry with Saul. Saul was discarded and David took over.

As time passed, the kingship passed on to Rehoboam, under whose leadership, Israel broke into two nations: Israel and Judah. The people of Israel were stubborn like God accused them of. They would not listen. God got angry and handed His chosen people—Israel to the Assyrians and Judah. He punished by handing them to Babylonians.

Fast-forward: The chosen people were massacred in the millions during the Second World War. God's chosen people. Did it pay to be the chosen people?

*And to this day, man sits there and blames himself. Man has concluded that his sin was the reason for his continuous punishment. And to this day, God too is yet to stop blaming man for his **mistakes**.*

Is this the All-knowing, Omnipotent, Omnipresent, Omniscient Creator? Or is He the God only man could create?

As I write this, I can't help but see group-think among many believers of the Holy Books. To group-think per se is not bad; after all, religions require that members group-think. But to group-think in an unthinking acceptance of majority opinions is unacceptable. Their ability to group-think is infectious and blindingly ignorant. They do this group-think so much, that they are willing to mangle the simple meanings of the books to suit their narrow-mindedness. When you object, they either blame the Greek, Hebrew, or Aramaic languages as one of the reasons it was difficult to translate the Bible into other later languages. They see logic where illogicality is aplenty.

What is group-think?—Group-think is conformity in thought and behavior among the members of a group, especially an unthinking acceptance of majority opinions. Group-think occurs when a homogenous, highly cohesive group is so concerned with maintaining unanimity that they fail to evaluate all their alternatives and options. Group-think members see themselves as part of an in-group working against a group considered as an outsider and which has opposing or contradictory goals. In group-think, faulty decisions are easily reached when compared to the decisions that could have been reached using an open, fair, and rational decision-making process.

Groups suffer from group-think if it overestimates its invulnerability or high moral stance, rationalizes the decisions it makes as a group, demonizes or stereotypes outside groups, and embraces a culture of uniformity where individuals censor themselves and others so that the facade of group unanimity is maintained. Group-think groups engage in, not making contingency plans if original plans fails, not seeking expert advice, and they always seem to select and use information that supports their conclusions.

You can now see the use of this concept of group-think in defending a belief in immutability. They create this façade that he cannot learn anything because learning something new implies change. If God cannot learn anything new, then there are things which God will never know, thereby conflicting with God's omniscient outlay of always knowing absolutely everything. If God is all those qualities, God's reaction in Genesis 6:1–7 was that mankind in general was deserving of God's destructive intervention into history through a flood. God's immutability took a nuclear-size blow for it would almost appear that God changed His mind, as though the creation of man was a colossal error on His part. That also would raise the question of just what the point of creation was. I can empathize with those many others who were influenced by Neoplatonism, especially in their identifying the Neoplatonic One, or God, with Yahweh. But, the above explanation is reason why many have not only rejected the doctrine that God is immutable, but also the general Neoplatonic argument that God must be perfect.

God is not a man, that He should lie, nor a son of man, that He should repent; has He said, and will He not do it? Or has He spoken, and will He not make it good? (Numbers 23:19)

And the Lord said to Moses, "I have seen this people, and behold, they are an obstinate people. Now then let Me alone, that My anger may burn against them, and that I may destroy them; and I will make of you a great nation." So the Lord changed His mind about the harm which He said He would do to His people (Exodus 32:9–10, 14).

"Let us always understand that man has God DNA and characteristics. Man's behaviors should not be a shock to anyone," Sam Oputa, page 117–120, Why Was Man Created?

At this juncture, are you not elated that countries/governments have the concept of separation of church and state? Let us take a look at why the United States chose this doctrine of a separation of church and state.

CHAPTER 17

Installing the Rule of Logic and Reason

NO DOUBTS, NO DAZZLE AND DELIGHT— THE SEPARATION OF DOCTRINES AND STATE

One of the best things to happen to United States of America is the concept of Separation of Church and State. Among the many things the Founding Fathers did, perhaps the separation of church and state laid the foundation for free will and freethinking. It did not portray any of the Founding Fathers as nonbelievers in God, but it laid a foundation for the proverbial "Give unto Caesar what is Caesar's" and unto United States what is hers. Looking back at that "give unto Caesar what belonged to Caesar's" statement credited to Christ, one can immediately see how smart and freethinking Jesus was/is.

The separation of church and state has thus reduced the contrasts and conflicts that would have unleashed religious anarchy on the state had this concept not been imposed. Even up to this day, this concept of separation of church and state put in place by our freethinking Founding Fathers has helped in no small way to resolve reoccurring clashes between law and religions. In an article, Kenneth Cauthen wrote, "Thorny problems arise in two particular areas. The first involves trying to steer between avoiding an establishment of religion and permitting its free exercise. Prayer in public schools is among the most contentious. Clearly state-sponsored prayer is forbidden, but at what point does student-initiated, voluntary prayer in connection with school activities cross the line? Is it legitimate for parents to use school vouchers from a state or local government to send their children to a religious school? The government-sponsored use of religious symbols in public places poses another set of dilemmas. Where is the dividing line between the religious and secular dimensions of certain Christmas symbols, for example, Christmas trees or a crèche? In 1984, the Supreme Court upheld a city-authorized Christmas display involving a crèche because it had mainly a secular purpose. Critics noted that this approval was made possible only by robbing the symbol of its sacred meaning. A second range of problems arises when religious belief and practice conflict with secular law. In 1878, the Supreme Court forbade the Mormon custom of polygamy because it is "an odious practice." In 1990, the Supreme Court ruled that members of the Native American Church did not have the right to the sacramental use of peyote, an illegal drug. Should an Orthodox Jew be allowed to wear a yarmulke while on duty in the military? The court said no. But at what point does state interest in outlawing reprehensible practices or merely having secular law prevail take precedence over religious freedom to obey God? All these conflicts occur between two spheres of authority and activity that are, in principle, separate but in practice sometimes overlap."

CHAPTER 18

Why You Have Doubts-1

The Bible is riddled with repetitions and contradictions—mostly as a result of fabrications, misinterpretations, and spin of the texts, things that the Bible critiques would be quick to point out in anything that they want to criticize. In opening up to the narratives for the possibilities and realizations of confusion, you, as a reader analyst, must allow self to be placed into the events and thus allow self to experience the story, rather than allowing the books of the Old Testament and sometimes New Testament to be an unrelenting temptress that draws the reader into indoctrination. We will concentrate on the books of Moses (the Pentateuch) and sometimes deviate to other books in the attempt to draw the reader/analyst really deep into the narratives.

This was a hip-hop narration of parts of the Old Testament. We will start with the book of Genesis, and this hip-hop version from the site shmoop.com is fun to read. Enjoy.

Book of Genesis: How It All Goes Down . . .

What's bigger, pound for pound: your phone book, your dictionary, or your Bible? Chances are your Bible stands a chance. It's pretty thick and scary-looking. But the good news is that Genesis is the easiest needle to find in this giant haystack because it's the very first book of the whole thing.

*The stories in Genesis can be best understood in two parts, Oreo cookie style. The first part is the prequel. It's about the origin of **everything** from why snakes slither on their bellies to why people speak different languages to how Superman found himself on earth. Okay, not that last one.*

The second part zooms in and is more narrowly focused on one family's long saga. A guy named Abraham is the Big Daddy of this clan, and we read all about what four generations of his descendants did after him. Seems basic enough, right? Well, it's pretty complex. There will be more names and locations in Genesis than in a Russian novel.

ZOOM OUT

*The first 11 chapters of Genesis are like a combination of creation myth, the **Star Wars** crawl, and a TV miniseries. Here's how it goes down:*

- *God creates the cosmos and humanity (**twice**, actually).*

- *Adam and Eve, the first humans, make cataclysmic (bad or good?) choices and get booted from the Garden of Eden.*

- *Their son Cain kills their other son Abel.*

- *Civilization at large becomes wicked. The bad kind.*

- *Noah, his family, and a numerically select group of animals are spared from a massive flood in order to restart creation.*

- *God "confuses" human speech by turning their one language into many, then scatters all people throughout the world. All because humanity tried to build a tower into the heavens. Silly humans, Trix are for kids.*

That's a lot for 11 chapters.

ZOOM IN

The rest of the book of Genesis (12:1–50:26) is a reality TV-style family saga told in old-fashioned biblical prose. The stories are generally about the patriarchs of the family (think Abraham, Isaac, and Jacob), but women like Sarah, Rebekah, Leah, and Rachel will get in on the action, too. Here are the details:

- *The deity sends Abraham to Canaan.*

- *The deity cuts two important deals with Abraham (Genesis 15, 17) promising a thriving lineage and land, meaning lots of kids and a place to put them for generations.*

- *Put **very** shortly, Abraham has two sons, Ishmael via Hagar and Isaac via Sarah. Isaac is much more important, even though he's the second born.*

- *Hospitality norms are breached by the male inhabitants in Sodom and Gomorrah. They try to rape the visitors. Result? God destroys the cities.*

- *Abraham rejects and expels Hagar and Ishmael into the wilderness.*

- *Abraham almost sacrifices Isaac at God's command.*

- *Isaac marries Rebekah, and they have twins: Esau the firstborn, then Jacob.*

- *Jacob, by aid of his mother, finagles his twin, Brother Esau's, birthright.*

- *Jacob acquires two brides, Leah and Rachel, by working for his uncle Laban. He has 12 sons and one daughter.*

- *The girl gets raped and her brothers wipe out a whole village in vengeance.*

- *Jacob's son Joseph is sold into slavery by his older brothers. Not cool.*

- *Sidebar: Tamar dupes her father-in-law Judah into having sex with her and getting her pregnant.*

- *As a slave in Egypt, Joseph gets sexually harassed, and then wrongfully accused of sexual assault. He's thrown in prison.*

- *Joseph interprets Pharaoh's dreams and goes from prisoner to CFO of Egypt in one day.*

- *A famine brings Joseph's brothers to Egypt.*

- *Joseph concocts a clever way to reveal himself to his brothers and gets some revenge on them for selling him into slavery by making them wiggle and worry.*

- *Jacob and his family move to Egypt, where Jacob blesses Joseph's son and shares his final words with his sons.*

- *Jacob dies. Joseph makes up with his brothers, and then he dies, too.*

We know. This is an absurd amount of information. It can be like getting caught up on all the family gossip over the holidays or sitting through an episode of Gossip Girl. *And you know what? We **love*** Gossip Girl.

CHAPTER 19

Why You Have Doubts-2

Let us now apply some of the concepts we have learned either through the sciences or other areas of studies. Genesis is the title given to the first book of Moses by its Greek translators. The word means "origin" or "beginning." Truly, Genesis is a book of beginnings. It describes the beginning of man and the universe which he inhabits, the beginning of sin, the consequent beginning of an effort at redemption, and the beginning of the Hebrew nation.

However, Genesis 1 and 2 disagree about the order in which things were created, and how satisfied God was about the results of His work. The Flood story was indeed really two interwoven stories that contradict each other on how many of each kind of animal were to be brought into the ark. It was not clear if it was a pair or seven pairs each of the clean animals that were to be taken into the ark. The book of Genesis describes the steps which led to the establishment of the theocracy. Two ideas are seen to be predominant in the Bible:

1. The people of God and the Promised Land. Genesis has a character which is both special and universal. The book, even while it embraced the entire world as it speaks of God as the God of mankind, seems to change the narrative's theme as soon as an introduction to Jewish history debuts.

2. The universal theme becomes subordinate to the nation of Israel. Its design is to show how God first revealed Himself to the patriarchs of the Hebrew race in order to make of them a people who are the chosen people of Yahweh.

3. Whether this will unite the peoples of earth or cause confusion is dependent on your take of the book. This, however, is the inner principle of unity which pervades the entire book.

Moses is claimed to have written the book of Genesis and others that made up the Pentateuch. How and where he received his information is questionable at best. The Bible explains how, where, and the time. We know where Yahweh met Moses for the first time and that was in the book of Exodus. Meanwhile, you may wish at this juncture to read the comparison of the Genesis creation narrative with that of the Sumerian text found in the Enuma Elish, and is very well explained in the book *Why Was Man Created?*

Genesis 1 is one of the foundational chapters in the entire Bible. It tells us how everything was started and establishes the basic teaching on who God is and who we are in reference to Him. There has been and will continue to be arguments about secondary issues like history and science, but Genesis 1 continues to turn the eyes of believers and nonbelievers alike up toward the heavens while marveling at the majesty of the God described in Genesis 1. The book of Genesis is where it all began, and as with the many books that comprise the Bible, Genesis has its many inconsistencies.

Bible scholars suggest that the book of Genesis was compiled from the writings of several different authors. Chapters 1 and 2, for example, were almost certainly written by different authors. That explains the confusion inherent in the creation narratives. The writing style is different, and the technique used for creation is different. For example, in chapter 1, creation was an act of will. God said let there be light and there was light; however, in chapter 2, creation becomes a hands-on process. God physically formed

Adam out of mud according to the texts. Though, it is said by some, that those who are well versed in Hebrew would tell us that the name of God is different in the two chapters, we can, on our own, find the very many names of God in subsequent chapters and narratives. Sometimes, He is Yahweh, El, Elohim, I am who I am, Jehovah, Jehovah Jireh, Jehovah Nissi, God of Abraham, Isaac, and Jacob, etc. There are so many names, but one name that stands out for this author is: ADONAI. This name stands out for me for so many reasons because, as I research the book in different versions, I noticed that some versions of the Bible seem to yank that name out and sometimes replace it. The work to unravel why this was so is ongoing. Again, while Genesis 1 is an overview of the creative days, chapter 2 was a backtrack to elucidate details on the creation of man. Personally, I hate to use the word "creation" of man, in chapter 2. In the book *Why Was Man Created?* I started using *reengineering* as opposed to creation of man because man was already created by the Universal Creator in Genesis 1.

CHAPTER 20

Why You Have Doubts-3

WHAT IS A CREATIVE DAY? ANOTHER CONFLICT OF INTERPRETATION:

Creative day 1—Divided day and night.

Day 2—Separating the waters

Day 3—Land appears and vegetation, trees and grass begin to grow

Day 4—The great luminaries appear

Day 5—Fish and birds created

Day 6—Animals and man created, "male and female he created them"

Day 7—God rested

The above is covered in Genesis 1:1–31. Below, I hope you will see the confusion as it starts to mount. In Genesis 2:5, we read "and before every plant of the field was in the earth, and before every herb of the field grew; for the Lord God had not caused it to rain upon the earth, and there was not a man to till the ground." Now there was as yet no bush of the field found in the earth and no vegetation of the field was as yet sprouting. This is because God has not made it rain and "there was no man to cultivate the ground."

So, this account has taken us back to day three of the creative period, before man was created and before vegetation was on the earth. Then, from Genesis 2:7–25, it explains more, detailing the creation of the first man and woman, Adam and Eve.

[7] And the Lord God formed man of the dust of the ground, and breathed into his nostrils the breath of life; and man became a living soul.

[8] And the Lord God planted a garden eastward in Eden, and there He put the man whom He had formed.

[9] And out of the ground made the Lord God to grow every tree that is pleasant to the sight and good for food, the tree of life also in the midst of the garden, and the tree of knowledge of good and evil.

[10] And a river went out of Eden to water the garden, and from thence it was parted and became four heads.

[11] The name of the first is Pishon; that is it which compasseth the whole land of Havilah, where there is gold.

[12] And the gold of that land is good, and there is bdellium and the onyx stone.

[13] And the name of the second river is Gihon; the same is it that compasseth the whole land of Cush.

[14] And the name of the third river is Hiddekel; that is it which goeth toward the east of Assyria. And the fourth river is Euphrates.

[15] And the Lord God took the man and put him into the Garden of Eden to dress it and to keep it.

[16] And the Lord God commanded the man, saying, "Of every tree of the garden thou mayest freely eat;

[17] but of the tree of the knowledge of good and evil, thou shalt not eat of it. For in the day that thou eatest thereof, thou shalt surely die."

¹⁸ And the Lord God said, "It is not good that the man should be alone; I will make him a helper meet for him."

¹⁹ And out of the ground the Lord God formed every beast of the field, and every fowl of the air, and brought them unto Adam to see what he would call them; and whatsoever Adam called every living creature, that was the name thereof.

²⁰ And Adam gave names to all cattle, and to the fowl of the air, and to every beast of the field; but for Adam there was not found a helper meet for him.

²¹ And the Lord God caused a deep sleep to fall upon Adam, and he slept; and He took one of his ribs, and closed up the flesh instead thereof.

²² And the rib which the Lord God had taken from man, made He a woman and brought her unto the man.

²³ And Adam said, "This is now bone of my bones, and flesh of my flesh; she shall be called Woman, because she was taken out of Man."

²⁴ Therefore shall a man leave his father and his mother, and shall cleave unto his wife; and they shall be one flesh.

²⁵ And they were both naked, the man and his wife, and were not ashamed.

Animals were created first, then man. But since they were both created in the same creative day, God was still creating animals after He created Adam and bringing them to Him to suggest and name them. However, Eve was the last creative work.

From the above, thus far, you can see the inconsistencies. Such inconsistencies could not have happened if there was one author. The Old Testament was written by more than one person. It was not only written by Moses as they would have you believe. It was compiled over several thousands of years, depending on the politics and circumstances of the writers at the time. It sounds like two different stories—creation of animals and the naming, then the creation of Eve. And, yes, it gets worse. Read Genesis carefully. . .

> [19] Now the LORD God had formed out of the ground all the beasts of the field and all the birds of the air . . .

> [20] But for Adam no suitable helper was found . . .

> [22] **Then the LORD God made a woman from the rib**

Does this suggest that God initially offered Adam animals, but since they were not suitable, He then did a Plan B and made a woman as helper for Adam? This is interesting. Meanwhile, do not forget that in Genesis 1 God made Adam and Eve at the same time, but in Genesis 2 He makes Adam first, and then after a search for a helper and not finding one for Adam among the animals, He decided to create Eve out of Adam's rib. You may wish to read or reread about the creation of Adam and Eve in Genesis 1 and more in chapter 2.

As one reads and rereads the Genesis creation stories you notice confusion like this one: God created light and separated light from the darkness, day from night. Meanwhile, He has not created such light making structures such as the sun, moon, and stars until the fourth day. Pay special attention to Genesis 1:3–5 & 1:14–19, but below, I reproduce Genesis 1:3–19.

> [3] And God said, "Let there be light"; and there was light.

> [4] And God saw the light, that it was good; and God divided the light from the darkness.

[5] And God called the light Day, and the darkness He called Night. And the evening and the morning were the first day.

[6] And God said, "Let there be a firmament in the midst of the waters, and let it divide the waters from the waters."

[7] And God made the firmament, and divided the waters which were under the firmament from the waters which were above the firmament; and it was so.

[8] And God called the firmament Heaven. And the evening and the morning were the second day.

[9] And God said, "Let the waters under the heaven be gathered together unto one place, and let the dry land appear"; and it was so.

[10] And God called the dry land Earth; and the gathering together of the waters called He Seas; and God saw that it was good.

[11] And God said, "Let the earth bring forth grass, the herb yielding seed, and the fruit tree yielding fruit after his kind, whose seed is in itself, upon the earth"; and it was so.

[12] And the earth brought forth grass, and herb yielding seed after his kind, and the tree yielding fruit, whose seed was in itself, after his kind; and God saw that it was good.

[13] And the evening and the morning were the third day.

[14] And God said, "Let there be lights in the firmament of the heaven to divide the day from the night; and let them be for signs and for seasons, and for days and years;

¹⁵ and let them be for lights in the firmament of the heaven to give light upon the earth"; and it was so.

¹⁶ And God made two great lights: the greater light to rule the day, and the lesser light to rule the night. He made the stars also.

¹⁷ And God set them in the firmament of the heaven to give light upon the earth,

¹⁸ and to rule over the day and over the night, and to divide the light from the darkness. And God saw that it was good.

¹⁹ And the evening and the morning were the fourth day.

God spends one-sixth of his entire creative effort (the second day) working on a solid firmament. This structure, God called heaven, is intended to separate the higher waters from the lower waters. This firmament, if it existed, would have been quite an obstacle to our space program. This firmament (heaven) which is supposed to hold the waters above (heaven) could have been a very big hindrance to NASA and its space program. Such heavenly waters would also hinder Brazil Airlines, British Airways, Singapore Airlines, EL AL Airlines, and other airlines and jets. But the confusion and inconsistencies continued.

There was the creation of plants on the third day prior to the creation of the sun. We now know the process of photosynthesis. He created the stars also. We now know something about the life and death of stars. All stars in our galaxy and in all galaxies use the process of nuclear fusion to create energy, light, and heat.

According to the creation stories, God spends a day making light (before making the stars) and separating light from darkness; then, at the end of a hard day's work, and almost as an afterthought, He makes trillions of stars (Genesis 1:16).

Lest I forget, let me quickly bring up this next quote, Genesis 1:28, where God commanded us to *Be fruitful and multiply, and replenish the earth, and subdue it; and have dominion over the fish of the sea, and over the fowl of the air, and over every living thing that moveth upon the earth.*

I bring this up because it has led some folks to use this line to justify Christian opposition to birth control, to lack of concern for the environment, and to question animal rights activists. They argue that the earth was made for humans, and they can do as they damn well please with it.

In Genesis, we learn that all animals were originally herbivores. Really? Genesis 1:29–31 states:

²⁹ And God said, "Behold, I have given you every herb bearing seed which is upon the face of all the earth, and every tree in which is the fruit of a tree yielding seed; to you it shall be for meat.

³⁰ And to every beast of the earth, and to every fowl of the air, and to every thing that creepeth upon the earth wherein there is life, I have given every green herb for meat"; and it was so.

³¹ And God saw every thing that He had made, and behold, it was very good. And the evening and the morning were the sixth day.

Yikes! So, tapeworms, worms of the nematode family, vampire bats, mosquitoes, and barracudas were all strict vegetarians. But, of course, we now know that there were carnivorous animals millions of years before humans existed.

We read in Genesis 3:8–11 that God walks and talks to self in the garden where he played hide-and-seek with Adam and Eve. We also read about a clever talking serpent, Gen. 3:1, that had an opportunity to be cursed, thus: *From now on the serpent will crawl on its belly and eat dust.* One wonders how the serpent moved around before. Did it possess legs before or did it move around by hopping on its tail? Do snakes eat dust now? Snakes still don't eat dust . . . or do they? (Verse 3:14) God curses the ground and causes thorns and thistles to grow (verse 3:17–18). God killed some animals and made some skin coats for Adam and Eve (verse 3:21).

Meanwhile, we read that Cain was worried after killing Abel when he said, "Every one who finds me shall slay me." Is this not confusing as it is strange? It is strange for Cain to have this fear since there were only two other humans alive at the time according to the texts—his parents (4:14).

Again, we read of Cain, "And Cain went out from the presence of the LORD" (4:16). "And Cain knew his wife." That is an incredibly confusing and yet a fantastic story, but where the hell did she (the wife) come from? (Verse 4:17) According to the texts, there was no mention of other humans. There were no other humans around unless the author (s)/God forgot to mention them if they had existed.

Genesis 4:23, And Lamech said unto his wives, "Adah and Zillah, hear my voice; ye wives of Lamech, hearken unto my speech! For I have slain a man for my wounding, and a young man for my hurt.

[24] If Cain shall be avenged sevenfold, truly Lamech seventy and sevenfold."

Does that not sound fair? Is this not rationalization of murder. Oh, OK, there was no law against murder then.

God created a man and a woman and called them both Adam. So the woman's name should be Adam too? (Genesis 5:2)

Then, the "sons of God" made love to the "daughters of men" and had children who became giants and men of valor and mighty men of renown (Genesis 6:2–4).

So God found out that human imagination is always evil. Remember the word immutability here. Christians like to throw that word around a lot. God decides to kill all living things because man's imagination is evil. (By the way, it was impossible to kill all living things. For example, fishes, bacteria, fungi, and other water animals.) But later in Genesis 8:21

He regrets His acts and promised never to behave that way again. Was this not erratic behavior? If it was not, I wonder what is. See Genesis 6:5–7.

In Genesis, Chapter 6:11–13, God is mad because the world is filled with violence. The question is, who created this messy system in the first place? God created them all—predator and the prey, parasite and host were all designed by God. Though, initially, God intended all animals to be vegetarians as in Genesis 1:30. Initially, all animals were herbivores, so claimed the Bible—the tapeworms, vampire bats, lions, mosquitoes, leeches, lice, chicken, snakes, barracudas—all were herbivores. Now we know that there were carnivorous animals millions of years before man was created.

Genesis 6:16, God asked Noah to make a window of about 18 inches in a 450 foot ark for ventilation. Is that sufficient with all the animals inside that ark?

Genesis 7:11, "God opens the windows of heaven." Does God do this every time it rains

Genesis 8:2, "God stopped the windows of heaven and the rain from heaven was restrained." Does God do this too every time it stopped raining?

Genesis 6:9 and 7:1, Noah is described as just and righteous.

Genesis 9:20–21, Noah is drunk and naked.

That God got mad is surprising because it was of His making. The most confusing part is that God thought that by killing off all living things, violence would have been eradicated. Was it? Did God think that by killing all animals, the remaining saved ones will suddenly behave less violently? Like Christians would say, "God works in miraculous ways." Life does not have plots. It has people and conflicts and growth. It has new information that allows one to grow further. And it has pain. Did this God not factor all these into the equation? If He did, which I presume He did, then He is impatient. If He did not factor all these into the equation, which seems more logical, then He was, and still is, NOT immutable.

Genesis 8:8–11, Noah sends out a dove to check if there was any dry land but none was found. Then, 7 days later, Noah repeated the same thing and the dove returned with a plant, an olive leaf. How is this possible? How could an olive tree survive the flood? Even if it was an olive seed that survived, it certainly could not have germinated and grown leaves in only 7 days.

Then Noah took of every clean animal and of every clean bird and offered burnt offerings on the altar. Now, according to Genesis 7:8–9, this would have caused the extinction of all clean animals since only two of each was taken onto the ark.

After the Lord had finished eating by "smelling a sweet savor," the Lord said in His heart that He would never destroy the world again with a flood because "Man's heart is filled with evil from his youth." Let us see that word again—immutability—that word that Christians love to toss all over the place when describing God's qualities. So God's excuse to have killed all living things is because humans are evil, and then again promises not to kill off living things again because man's heart is evil. Or did man suddenly acquire a clean mind? God's mind is never to be understood by sinful man. Is there even a difference between God's thinking mind and that of man?

Genesis 11:4

God worries that man could actually build a tower high enough to reach Him in heaven. Unless heaven is not where we think it is or heaven is not what we imagine it to be—in the skies—is it not awesome that God could think that man could build a tower to reach Him?

Did it ever occur to anyone that maybe God, when He was on earth, resided on the mountains somewhere in the present-day Middle East? For man to build a structure as tall as the mountains is for man to stand in his tower and snoop through cognizance around God's movements and doings. Obviously, God did not want that. The secrets had to be protected.

After all, this same God worried before. Remember how humans nearly became gods by eating of the fruit of knowledge of good and evil? And how He worried that humans could become gods by finding and eating there from the tree of life in Genesis 3:22? Oh no! God has to do something to stop mankind. God was not scared of mankind. He was just worried. But He fears that . . . Genesis 11:6, "now nothing will be restrained from them, which they have imagined to do" because the people is one and they all have one language.

Today, if a person lives up to 70, such a person has lived long and would look feeble and weak. But according to the Bible, people lived longer lives then. Did you ever wonder that at 70, Sarai, Abram's wife, was still making kings squirm at the sight of her? The Pharaoh could not resist her as narrated in Genesis 12:11–16.

[11] And it came to pass, when he had come near to enter into Egypt that he said unto Sarai his wife, "Behold now, I know that thou art a fair woman to look upon.

[12] Therefore it shall come to pass, when the Egyptians shall see thee, that they shall say, 'This is his wife'; and they will kill me, but they will save thee alive.

[13] Say, I pray thee, thou art my sister, that it may be well with me for thy sake, and my soul shall live because of thee."

[14] And it came to pass, when Abram had come into Egypt, that the Egyptians beheld the woman, that she was very fair.

[15] The princes also of Pharaoh saw her, and commended her before Pharaoh; and the woman was taken into Pharaoh's house.

[16] And he treated Abram well for her sake; and he had sheep and oxen and heasses, and menservants and maidservants, and sheasses and camels.

In Genesis 14:7 and 36:12, Amalekites were slaughtered and smitten before Amalek was born. Amalekites are the descendants of Amalek, the grandson of Esau.

In Genesis 17:23–24, Abraham circumcises himself and all the males in his household. Here we can figure out how important penises are to Yahweh. If God so hated foreskins, and if He created men, why, then, did He create penises with foreskins? This God definitely knows how to complain about His work. Did He not think about it and plan accordingly? Yet, He kept complaining.

    a.   He complained and regrets creating man.

    b.   He complains man is nothing but hopelessly sinful in nature.

    c.   He committed mass murder and recognized His immutability, then creates the rainbow as a sign to remind Him and living things never to commit such wickedness again. Is He that forgetful? Man is probably not safe from a forgetful God such as Yahweh.

    d.   Now, He complains about man's penises. When would He take responsibility for His mistakes in creation? Again, the book already admonished us not to ask silly questions.

In Genesis 18:11–14, Sarah, who was about 90 years and has gone through menopause, laughs when she heard God say that she will bear a son. God assured her that when the appropriate time comes He will be there to make her tummy big with child. The part that is interesting is that the Bible says what God will do and that He will be there to do it. But some very, very holy people will not interpret this verse as is. It is not as if the Bible has not described that "sons of God" were making out with women. They (sons of God) did not just come to earth and suddenly developed a "craving" for coitus. If only I had the luxury of space and limitless word count, I would have gone into narration of the various rationalizations used to explain away Genesis 6:4. If you must read some of them, they are found in the book *Why Was Man Created?*

From Genesis 21:1–2, we read that the Lord visited Sarah as He had said, and did for her as He had spoken.

In Genesis 35:10, God renames Jacob for the first time, yet Jacob is still referred to as Jacob in later days, even by God as in Genesis 46:2.

Jacob wrestles with God and prevails. Jacob prevailed over God? you might ask. Oh yes, so says the Bible. Genesis 32:24–30. And God changes Jacob's name to Israel. Why name and rename Jacob more than once? Obviously, the name did not stick well the first time.

Genesis Chapter 36 is all about genealogy. Remember 1 Timothy 1:4 and Titus 3:9, where we were asked to not bother about this? So, how come the Bible is contradicting the Bible?

Genesis 19:30–38:

[30] And Lot went up out of Zoar and dwelt on the mountain, and his two daughters with him, for he feared to dwell in Zoar; and he dwelt in a cave, he and his two daughters.

[31] And the firstborn said unto the younger, "Our father is old, and there is not a man on the earth to come in unto us after the manner of all the earth.

[32] Come, let us make our father drink wine, and we will lie with him, that we may preserve seed of our father."

[33] And they made their father drink wine that night, and the firstborn went in and lay with her father; and he perceived not when she lay down, nor when she arose.

[34] And it came to pass on the morrow that the firstborn said unto the younger, "Behold, I lay yesternight with my father. Let us make him drink wine this night also, and go thou in and lie with him, that we may preserve seed of our father."

³⁵ And they made their father drink wine that night also. And the younger arose and lay with him; and he perceived not when she lay down, nor when she arose.

³⁶ Thus were both the daughters of Lot with child by their father.

³⁷ And the firstborn bore a son and called his name Moab; the same is the father of the Moabites unto this day.

³⁸ And the younger, she also bore a son and called his name Benammi; the same is the father of the children of Ammon unto this day.

This is the same Lot who was described as just and righteous in 2 Peter 2:6–10. Is the amount of alcohol that knocked Lot out for his daughters to take advantage of him not strong enough to knock his sexual abilities out? Are you surprised? Is this not the same Lot who offered the same daughters for sex to would-be angel rapers? (Genesis 19:8)

Genesis 21:14–18 suggests that Ishmael was an infant when Sarah demanded he and his mother Hagar be cast out. But according to Genesis 17:25 and 21:5–8, he must have been at least 16 years old. Would it not have been tough for Hagar to carry a 16-year-old Ishmael on her back or shoulder and to "cast him under one of the shrubs" (Genesis 21:14–18)?

Abraham names the place where he almost sacrificed Isaac after Jehovah (Genesis 22:14). However, Exodus 6:3 seems to disagree as it suggests that Abraham could not have known God by the name Jehovah.

Jacob names Bethel for the first time before knowing/meeting Rachel (Genesis 28:19) and again in Genesis 35:15, just before Rachel died. So, Bethel as a name did not stick the first time?

Sexual behaviors then: Why would God tell Jacob's premarriage story like that? Are we supposedly to learn some morals from it? Let us regurgitate the story once more. Jacob goes in and had an overnight sexual marathon with Leah by mistake, then wakes up in the morning after the overnight exercise to complain to Laban that he was deceived. Was he drunk? Such stories!

Jacob went in unto Bilhah. And Bilhah conceived and bore a son for Jacob (Genesis 30:4).

And Leah, not to be outdone, gives Zilpah (her maid) to Jacob. And Zilpah bare Jacob a son (Genesis 30:9). Apart from the exhibition of such sex extravaganzas, it seems all portrayal of arranged sex has as its fruit of the loins a baby son. The chance of arranged sex whether between mankind and other beings simply do not yield baby daughters except in verse 21 where Leah gave birth to a daughter, Dinah.

In Genesis 30:15–16, we see, [15] But she said unto her, "Is it a small matter that thou hast taken my husband? And wouldest thou take away my son's mandrakes also?" And Rachel said, "Therefore he shall lie with thee tonight, for thy son's mandrakes."

[16] And Jacob came out of the field in the evening, and Leah went out to meet him and said, "Thou must come in unto me, for surely I have hired thee with my son's mandrakes." And he lay with her that night.

So, Rachel trades some of Jacob's favors for some mandrakes, and so when Jacob came home, Leah said, "Thou must come in unto me, for surely I have hired thee with my son's mandrakes." And he slept with her that night. Talk about sex for sale even among the married! Presumably, God told this "edifying" story to teach us something about sexual ethics.

Anyway, the Bible is self-advising when it comes to matters such as the above for in the book of 1 Timothy 1:1–4, it advised,

1 Paul, an apostle of Jesus Christ by the commandment of God our Savior, and Lord Jesus Christ, who is our hope,

[2] Unto Timothy, my own son in the faith: Grace, mercy, and peace from God our Father and Jesus Christ our Lord.

[3] As I besought thee when I went into Macedonia to abide still at Ephesus, that thou mightest charge some that they teach no other doctrine,

[4] neither give heed to fables and endless genealogies, which promote questions rather than godly edifying in the faith, so do!

AND

Titus 3:9, But avoid foolish questions, and genealogies, and contentions, and strivings about the law, for they are unprofitable and vain.

CHAPTER 21

Why You Have Doubts-4

Meanwhile, as we move into the book, Exodus, the Bible continues to edify through narration and imagery, the powers of God. The Greek translators called this book Exodus—which signifies a departure or going out—because it begins with the story of the going out of the children of Israel from Egypt. Some allude to the names of this and the foregoing book, and observe that immediately after Genesis, which signifies the beginning or original, it follows Exodus, which signifies a departure. It is the summary of the book that told how the children of Israel left slavery in Egypt through the strength of Yahweh, the God who, according to the book, has chosen Israel as His people. Led by their prophet Moses, they journey through the wilderness to Mount Sinai, where Yahweh promises them the land of Canaan—the Promised Land—in return for their faithfulness. Israel enters into a covenant with Yahweh who gives them their laws and instructions for the Tabernacle, the means by which He will dwell with them and lead them to the land, and give them peace.

Some Bible scholars have described the book of Exodus in the following words. As the book of Genesis narrated how the earth was, in the beginning, first fetched from under water, and then beautified and replenished, so Israel was first, by an almighty power, made to emerge out of Egyptian slavery, and then enriched with God's law and tabernacle.

But then, did the Exodus really happen? Some disagree. There are those who are convinced that Exodus was a narration of fiction in edification of a local god so as to elevate that god. They hinge their argument on lack of archaeological finds. And even where such finds are available, the study of archaeology is brought to question as we read in this article, "While people don't usually get worked up about archaeology, the debate about archaeology and the Bible is often passionate and vitriolic. Biblical archaeology is often divided into two camps: The 'minimalists' tend to downplay the historical accuracy of the Bible, while the 'maximalists,' who are in the majority and are, by and large, not religious, tend to suggest that archaeological evidence supports the basic historicity of the Bible text. As a science, we must understand what archaeology is and what it isn't. Archaeology consists of two components: the excavation of ancient artifacts, and the interpretation of those artifacts. While the excavation component is more of a mechanical skill, the interpretive component is very subjective. Presented with the same artifact, two world-class archaeologists will often come to different conclusions—particularly when ego, politics, and religious beliefs enter the equation." The article was in a *Los Angeles Times* publication and was titled, "Doubting the Story of Exodus," asserting that archaeology disproves the validity of the biblical account.

Some are quick to suggest that the event, if it happened, should have been very important for the writers of the book of Exodus to name the Pharaoh under whose reign the event took place. It has been suggested that if the event was so important, the Egyptians would have recorded such a historical event, especially the plagues, and the particularly the last plague. They dug into history to prove that at this period, Egypt was under a peaceful and prosperous reign, perhaps at the zenith of her power. That would suggest that mass emigration was improbable at such a time. They went into history to match geographical mentions in the Exodus story and matched basically none of the towns mentioned in the story. Whether the exodus described in the book of Exodus even occurred, or whether part of this thinking is due to lack of archaeological evidence, some still assert that the exodus as described was impossible given the sheer number of people involved. Therefore, many scholars argue that there was no "mass exodus," but rather a long-term migration in "bits" from Egypt to the Promised Land.

For even among those who believe that a mass exodus did occur, there is still a debate over whether it occurred earlier or later. The dates of the event have become even as contentious as the event/nonevent itself. Some believe that it occurred under the Egyptian pharaoh Amenhotep II, who ruled from 1450 to 1425 BCE, while others believe that it occurred under Ramses II, who ruled from 1290 to 1224 BCE.

Apart from the Israelites whose exodus was not mentioned or yet to be found in the scribbles of Egypt, it should be mentioned that many peoples in different African nations today claim the exodus from Egypt. Their events were not all recorded in Egypt's artifacts. Therefore, that Israel's exodus was not mentioned is nothing unique. However, if, according to the Bible, Pharaoh and his army were drowned in the sea, that the record of such death of a Pharaoh and his army through drowning was not mentioned in history seems very odd and absurd. Admittedly, however, if there is a shortage of Egyptian documentation of the Moses Exodus and the other exoduses, there must be a reason. In determining those reasons, we need to understand how the ancient world viewed the whole idea of recording history. The vast majority of inscriptions found in the ancient Egypt/Middle Eastern world had a specific agenda. That agenda was to glorify the deeds of the kings and to show their full military power and conquests. That there was an exodus of such magnitude as that described in the Bible brings no glory to the Pharaoh. If anything, the exodus edified and continues to edify Yahweh—the being who introduced Himself to Moses the first time in the book of Exodus.

According to an article by Austine Cline from about.com, we cull the following: *"Traditionally the authorship of the Book of Exodus was ascribed to Moses, but scholars began to reject that in the 19th century.*

With the development of the documentary hypothesis the scholarly view on who wrote Exodus has settled around an early version being written by the Yahwist author in the Babylonian exile of the 6th century BCE and the final form being put together in the 5th century BCE. The earliest version of Exodus probably wasn't written any earlier than the 6th century BCE, during the exile in Babylon. Exodus was probably in its final form, more or less, by the 5th century BCE, but some believe that revisions continued down through the 4th century BCE."

To deeply and historically go into the book of Exodus will perhaps be a work for some other time; however, let us make a few more points here.

Imagine two million migrants leaving Egypt at the same time. In the wilderness, even as ten abreast while marching forward, they would have formed a 120-mile human line. Even at 20 human abreast, that will still form 60 miles. Bearing this imagery in mind, then ask further questions. How did Moses communicate in an instant to all of the emigrants what Yahweh demanded of them? The message must have some noise in its transmission because obviously the message must transmit/transfer/travel from one group to the next until a 120/60 mile radius was covered. That obviously would take nights and days to accomplish. And we all know how communication gets after three transmissions through three different groups.

However, there were, and still are, nations of peoples in Africa today who claim Egyptian ancestry. They narrate how their forefathers emigrated from Egypt and how some of their customs followed practices of ancestral Egypt. If these other emigrants departed from Egypt successfully, communications noise or not, then the Israelites could have pull off the same feat. Of course, yes, but those other emigrants are not under scrutiny here; neither did they promote a god.

Meanwhile let us recall how the story unfolded briefly and note a very significant observation. One day, nearly 40 years after he first fled to the wilderness of Midian, Moses led his flock toward Mount Sinai, where he noticed a strange apparition—a bush was burning but was not consumed by the fire. When Moses turned aside to take a closer look, God suddenly began to speak to him: "Moses, Moses . . . do not come nearer; take your shoes off your feet, for the place on which you are standing is holy ground" (Exod. 3:4–5).

Exodus 3:1–6:

3 Now Moses kept the flock of Jethro his father-in-law, the priest of Midian; and he led the flock to the back side of the desert and came to the mountain of God, even to Horeb.

² And the angel of the Lord appeared unto him in a flame of fire out of the midst of a bush; and he looked and, behold, the bush burned with fire, and the bush was not consumed.

³ And Moses said, "I will now turn aside and see this great sight, why the bush is not burnt."

⁴ And when the Lord saw that he turned aside to see, God called unto him out of the midst of the bush and said, "Moses, Moses." And he said, "Here am I."

⁵ And He said, "Draw not nigh hither. Put off thy shoes from off thy feet, for the place whereon thou standest is holy ground."

⁶ Moreover He said, "I am the God of thy father, the God of Abraham, the God of Isaac, and the God of Jacob." And Moses hid his face, for he was afraid to look upon God.

This chapter of the Bible authoritatively informs us about the first meeting of God and Moses. If this was the first meeting, and we have been schooled to accept that Moses wrote the book of Genesis, where and how did Moses get his information? This is a valid question, especially now that we know that texts existed that had the same creation narratives.

If Moses was the author of Genesis, he sure forgot to tell us that Yahweh narrated Genesis. For a clearer understanding of this sort of inquiry, you may want to read the book, *Why Was Man Created?*

As with Genesis, let us look at some verses that make a free flow of communication difficult, confusing, and noisy. It is such confusion that leads many interpreters to plug in the holes while employing self-fabricated contents.

In Exodus 4:3–4, God teaches Moses some magic tricks. He explained to Moses how to impress the Pharaoh. First, cast your rod on the ground and it would turn into a snake. Then, grab the snake by its tail and it will turn back into a rod.

Second, God asks Moses to make his hand appear leprous, and then cure it.

The tale continued. If those two tricks do not persuade the Pharaoh then there were more tricks to rattle Pharaoh. Moses was to pour water on the floor and turn it into blood. That must do it for the unyielding king. Wait, I thought He was all-knowing . . .

As per Yahweh's behavioral pattern of nonnegotiation, nonyielding, no-nonsense, my way or the highway leader that He is, how logical was it that soon after recruiting Moses as a mouthpiece, He wants to kill him?

Exodus 4:24 explains, "And it came to pass, on the way at the inn, that the Lord met him and sought to kill him" (KJV Online edition).

> 25 Then Zipporah took a sharp stone and cut off the foreskin of her son, and cast it at his feet and said, "Surely a bloody husband art thou to me."

> 26 So He let him go; then she said, "A bloody husband thou art, because of the circumcision."

In another edition of the Bible, the King James Version, has chapter 4:24 stating, "And it came to pass on the way, at the encampment, that the LORD met him and sought to kill him."

Why was God so possessed about the appearance of penises? He almost killed Moses over the look of a penis. Yahweh does not play when it comes to appearance of a penis. This is very interesting. It is interesting because He tends to detest a penis with foreskin. If He so detested such penises that much, why did He create man with a penis covered with foreskin? Is this a clue that He had nothing and no say in the creation of man? Hold on to this piece of information as it will come in handy when and if you read the book, *Why Was Man Created?*

In Exodus 7:9–13, God gives Moses and Aaron a heads-up, that when Pharaoh asks for a miracle, they should cast the rod on the ground and it would become a serpent. And so it was. But the Egyptian magicians performed the same trick. Yikes. How can the Egyptian magician perform a trick as that of a God? There must be something that we were not being told. However, Moses' snake swallowed Egypt's snake.

Exodus 7:1 is more telling than people see. The verse, perhaps, say a great deal about this God, Yahweh, than we want to accept and believe. The verse says, And the Lord said unto Moses, "See, I have made thee a god to Pharaoh, and Aaron thy brother shall be thy prophet."

Moses performs a few tricks and suddenly he is like a god to Pharaoh and Aaron his prophet. This surmises the modus operandi of God. Perform a few magic tricks of shock and awe to a group of persons who do not know any better and they call such acts—"miracles." And the people having not experienced such ever before had to design a name for such being(s). That they chose Elohim or God is not spectacular. It was just a thing to do.

Meanwhile, after the snake trick which the Egyptian magicians duplicated, God instructs Moses to turn the river into blood. And yet again, the Egyptian magicians duplicated the trick. This is not the problem. The problem is what or which river did the Egyptians turn to blood since the river is already bloody from Moses' magic? The Bible did not provide logical answers here, so we are left to plug in whatever imaginary story or event as the reader deems fit (Exodus 7:17–24).

Next was the plague of the frogs. Yet again, the Egyptian magicians duplicated this feat. Question: Where did the Egyptians learn their magic? Who taught the Egyptians magic? Before you think of any answers to these questions, let us ask, "Did the Egyptian magicians wait for Moses' frogs to be cleared out of Egypt before they made Pharaoh's frogs?" So far, it is 3–3, a draw. Can you imagine magicians holding God to a plague draw? (Exodus 8:2–7)

The next plague was lice afflicting man and beast. This plague was unique in that it started the avalanche of plagues the magicians could not duplicate. You may wonder if duplicating frogs was possible and lice impossible. It will be a very logical question if you asked such.

In the fifth plague, all the cattle in Egypt died (Exodus 9:6), but in same chapter, verses 19–20 and 22–26, God killed the livestock again.

The eight plagues had locusts that are so thick they enveloped the face of the whole earth (Exodus 10:4–6). By "covered the face of the whole earth," does the Bible mean "as far as the eyes can see"? This is important because if "by face of the whole earth," does that include the Antarctica? By referencing that, we are referring to the coldest spots on the planet then.

The whopper of the plagues is the ninth one. Here, there was darkness all over the land, yet within this same land where Israelites dwelt, there was light for them. This darkness must be "smart" darkness, knowing how to detect an Israelite from an Egyptian (Exodus 10:21–23).

Soon after the children of Israel took flight from Egypt following the plagues, the Egyptians chased after them with all the Pharaoh's horses. Did the Bible not tell us earlier in Exodus 9:3–6 that all the livestock were killed in an earlier plague? Please refer to Exodus 14:23.

In Exodus 24:10, "and they saw the God of Israel. And there was under His feet as it were a paved work of a sapphire stone, and as it were the body of heaven in his clearness."

Have you read the book, *God Is Not Enough, Messiah Needed*? In that book, you would see the explanation of "heaven" and other imageries.

In Exodus 28:33–36, Aaron was commanded to wear a bell whenever he enters the holy place. Failure to adhere to this rule will incur death. God would kill Aaron. The saying "belling the cat" comes to mind here. Why must Aaron wear a bell? Probably to announce his presence least he catches God unawares? Think about it.

In Exodus 34:14, God says His name is JEALOUS. I have never heard any pastor refer to Yahweh with this name.

Now, it has been established that the God of Israel demonstrated some serious unexplainable phenomena here and there. That this God can perform what appears to humans as a miracle was thoroughly established in the Bible. That the Egyptian magicians could perform some of this same magic is a work worth exploring. That work is, however, reserved for another day. The biblical God of the Israelites was/is portrayed as powerful, having the ability to cause Egyptian cattle to die while the Israelite cattle remained safe and healthy, caused the firstborn child of Egypt to die, inflicted serious bodily disease on the Egyptians, and most especially the toll of war while seeking a settlement for the children of Abraham was high. That that journey took Yahweh 40 years to accomplish does not portray an efficient leader or general of the Jewish army. If anything, it portrays Him as highly mutable, a throwback at a claim of immutability.

It therefore forces me to ask: Would it not have been cheaper and more efficient to just annihilate or chase out the Egyptians from their land and let the children of God inherit it? Is that not the exact modus operandi He applied on the Philistines? Thus, that modus operandi would have saved some lives (Israelites, Philistines, Amorites, Edomites, Anaks, etc.) If you argue that Yahweh was taking Israel to a land flowing with milk and honey (whatever that means), the land of Israel today is not flowing with that geographical region's milk: oil. If anything, Egypt was the land flowing with "milk and honey" at that time. Two funny questions I read on the Internet (Yahoo) by someone with a pseudonym Michael Tate, in his own words, goes like this: "Why does God not just do what He wants to have done? If He can bring the plagues and part the Red Sea (through Moses), then why not just make the Israelites disappear from Egypt and reappear in Israel?" The questions are valid because Yahweh can do anything He wants to do. At least that was how He is portrayed. He is God.

But then, the Bible always has a buffer. That buffer was presented as advice in Titus 3:9.

⁹ But avoid foolish questions, and genealogies, and contentions, and strivings about the law, for they are unprofitable and vain.

Yahweh's modus operandi at all times, described in the Old Testament, was "kill and be done with it." It was, and probably still is, His way or the death way. In His leadership style, there was no room for negotiation. His only known method of negotiation was through the covenants. Covenants He comes up with, with occasional updates. These covenants were simply the framework of the dos and don'ts of his requirements. There was no room for negotiation, but there was room to explain punishments for violating the covenants.

That Yahweh did not employ His method of operation in dealing with Pharaoh and his subjects was interesting, surprising, and confusing. It could be an exercise worth pursuing later to understanding the constraints why He abandoned His operational style. If you thoroughly read the Old Testament and put a finger on Yahweh's behavior pattern, you too would wonder why Egyptians were spared the instant judgment. Hint: Egypt was flourishing under the pharaohs' gods. Do you remember the Us in Let Us make man" request? Ok.

CHAPTER 22

Why You Have Doubts-5

In the book of Leviticus, there is something worth mentioning, notwithstanding the ritualistic bloody contents of it. In chapter 4:2, it says, "Speak unto the children of Israel, saying, 'If a soul shall sin through ignorance against any of the commandments of the Lord concerning things which ought not to be done, and shall do against any of them . . .'"

The question I have is how can a person sin unintentionally? OK, let us logically think that this means "Ignorance is no excuse under the law" theme of modern laws. But this sinning-while-ignorant theme was repeated in chapter 4:13, 22, 27, and chapter 5:15, 17. What this means is that an individual can commit a trespass without knowing it. For example, we all (mankind) will be unintentionally/ignorantly committing trespasses according to Leviticus 5:1–32. Are there men and women observing this law today?

Reproduced below is chapter 15. It is that important that we read it very carefully in full.

1 And the Lord spoke unto Moses and to Aaron, saying,

² "Speak unto the children of Israel, and say unto them, 'When any man hath a running issue out of his flesh, because of his issue he is unclean.

³ And this shall be his uncleanness in his issue: whether his flesh run with his issue or his flesh be stopped from running with his issue, it is his uncleanness.

⁴ Every bed whereon he lieth who hath the issue is unclean, and everything whereon he sitteth shall be unclean.

⁵ And whosoever toucheth his bed shall wash his clothes and bathe himself in water, and be unclean until the evening.

⁶ And he that sitteth on any thing whereon he sat who hath the issue shall wash his clothes and bathe himself in water, and be unclean until the evening.

⁷ And he that toucheth the flesh of him that hath the issue shall wash his clothes and bathe himself in water, and is unclean until the evening.

⁸ And if he that hath the issue spit upon him that is clean, then he shall wash his clothes and bathe himself in water, and be unclean until the evening.

⁹ And what saddle soever he rideth upon who hath the issue shall be unclean.

¹⁰ And whosoever toucheth any thing that was under him shall be unclean until the evening; and he that beareth any of those things shall wash his clothes and bathe himself in water, and be unclean until the evening.

¹¹ And whomsoever he toucheth who hath the issue and hath not rinsed his hands in water, he shall wash his clothes and bathe himself in water, and be unclean until the evening.

[12] And the vessel of earth that he toucheth who hath the issue shall be broken, and every vessel of wood shall be rinsed in water.

[13] "'And when he that hath an issue is cleansed of his issue, then he shall number to himself seven days for his cleansing, and wash his clothes, and bathe his flesh in running water, and shall be clean.

[14] And on the eighth day he shall take for himself two turtledoves or two young pigeons, and come before the Lord unto the door of the tabernacle of the congregation, and give them unto the priest.

[15] And the priest shall offer them, the one for a sin offering and the other for a burnt offering; and the priest shall make an atonement for him before the Lord for his issue.

[16] "'And if any man's seed of copulation go out from him, then he shall wash all his flesh in water and be unclean until the evening.

[17] And every garment and every skin whereon is the seed of copulation, shall be washed with water and be unclean until the evening.

[18] The woman also with whom a man shall lie with seed of copulation, they shall both bathe themselves in water and be unclean until the evening.

[19] "'And if a woman have an issue and her issue from her flesh be blood, she shall be put apart seven days; and whosoever toucheth her shall be unclean until the evening.

[20] And every thing that she lieth upon in her separation shall be unclean; every thing also that she sitteth upon shall be unclean.

²¹ And whosoever toucheth her bed shall wash his clothes and bathe himself in water, and be unclean until the evening.

²² And whosoever toucheth any thing that she sat upon shall wash his clothes and bathe himself in water, and be unclean until the evening.

²³ And if it be on her bed or on any thing whereon she sitteth, when he toucheth it, he shall be unclean until the evening.

²⁴ And if any man lie with her at all and her monthly discharge be upon him, he shall be unclean seven days; and all the bed whereon he lieth shall be unclean.

²⁵ "'And if a woman have an issue of her blood many days out of the time of her separation, or if it run beyond the time of her separation, all the days of the issue of her uncleanness shall be as the days of her separation; she shall be unclean.

²⁶ Every bed whereon she lieth all the days of her issue shall be unto her as the bed of her separation; and whatsoever she sitteth upon shall be unclean, as the uncleanness of her separation.

²⁷ And whosoever toucheth those things shall be unclean, and shall wash his clothes and bathe himself in water, and be unclean until the evening.

²⁸ But if she be cleansed of her issue, then she shall number to herself seven days, and after that she shall be clean.

²⁹ And on the eighth day she shall take unto her two turtledoves or two young pigeons, and bring them unto the priest to the door of the tabernacle of the congregation.

³⁰ And the priest shall offer one for a sin offering and the other for a burnt offering; and the priest shall make an atonement for her before the Lord for the issue of her uncleanness.

³¹ "'Thus shall ye separate the children of Israel from their uncleanness, that they die not in their uncleanness when they defile My tabernacle that is among them.'"

³² This is the law of him that hath an issue, and of him whose seed goeth from him and is defiled therewith,

³³ and of her that is sick with her monthly discharge, and of him that hath an issue, of the man and of the woman, and of him that lieth with her that is unclean.

Obviously, if Yahweh created man, He made a lot of mistakes because at every turn He finds fault with His creation. That the biological workings of the body suddenly make an individual unclean is interesting. Did Yahweh actually create man? It is as if He had no say or input in the creation of man. Read *Why Was Man Created?* to learn more about mankind's creation. If by "unclean" was meant hygiene, then that would be logical. But then, we must take the advice in Titus 3:9, "But avoid foolish questions, and genealogies, and contentions, and strivings about the law, for they are unprofitable and vain." Who do you think created man?

Even trees and their fruits could be uncircumcised too. We read in Leviticus 19:23–25:

²³ "'And when ye shall come into the land and shall have planted all manner of trees for food, then ye shall count the fruit thereof as uncircumcised. Three years shall it be as uncircumcised unto you. It shall not be eaten of.

²⁴ But in the fourth year all the fruit thereof shall be holy with which to praise the Lord.

²⁵ And in the fifth year shall ye eat of the fruit thereof, that it may yield unto you the increase thereof:

Meanwhile, the burning of a human alive with fire did not start recently. As heinous as the burning of a human is, it did not start today. It is a practice stipulated and learned from the Bible.

In chapter 21:9, we read an instruction to punish any daughter of a priest who prostitutes. ⁹ And the daughter of any priest, if she profane herself by playing the whore, she profaneth her father. She shall be burned with fire." Yikes!

There is more. According to Yahweh, descendants of Aaron who are handicapped one way or another were forbidden, according to Leviticus 21:16–21, from coming near offerings made to the LORD. The blind, hunchbacks, men with crooked eyes, broken hands or legs, eczema, scabs, or a eunuch cannot come near to offer the offerings made by fire to the LORD.

Today, Christian priests preside over last rites to the dead. They must be doing something unclean as Yahweh had decreed in chapter 21:11, neither shall he go in to any dead body, nor defile himself for his father or for his mother.

Some unclean acts the man of today commits, either knowingly or ignorantly, would have resulted in capital punishment in yesteryears. For example, in chapters 21:18, 21:20, 22:3–5, we read:

¹⁸ "For whatsoever man he be that hath a blemish, he shall not approach: a blind man, or a lame, or he that hath a flat nose, or any thing superfluous . . ." Flat nose? That means most people of color and of African descent today would not be allowed near the altar of God. Bishop Tutu of South Africa could not have come near God's altar. Sorry, Oprah Winfrey, James Brown—the godfather. Who knows, Michael Jackson may have read these portions of the book of Leviticus and thus fixed himself.

Below is the full reproduced quote of Leviticus 21 (KJV) online:

21 And the Lord said unto Moses, Speak unto the priests the sons of Aaron, and say unto them: 'There shall none be defiled for the dead among his people,

[2] except for his kin who is near unto him, that is: for his mother, and for his father, and for his son, and for his daughter, and for his brother,

[3] and for his sister, a virgin who is nigh unto him, who hath had no husband; for her may he be defiled.

[4] But he shall not defile himself, being a chief man among his people, to profane himself.

[5] They shall not make baldness upon their head, neither shall they shave off the corner of their beard nor make any cuttings in their flesh.

[6] They shall be holy unto their God and not profane the name of their God, for the offerings of the Lord made by fire and the bread of their God they do offer; therefore they shall be holy.

[7] They shall not take a wife who is a whore or profane, neither shall they take a woman put away from her husband; for he is holy unto his God.

[8] Thou shalt sanctify him therefore, for he offereth the bread of thy God. He shall be holy unto thee; for I the Lord, who sanctify you, am holy.

[9] And the daughter of any priest, if she profane herself by playing the whore, she profaneth her father. She shall be burned with fire.

[10] And he that is the high priest among his brethren, upon whose head the anointing oil was poured and who is consecrated to put on the garments, shall not uncover his head nor rend his clothes;

[11] neither shall he go in to any dead body, nor defile himself for his father or for his mother;

[12] neither shall he go out of the sanctuary nor profane the sanctuary of his God, for the crown of the anointing oil of his God is upon him: I am the Lord.

[13] And he shall take a wife in her virginity.

[14] A widow or a divorced woman or profane or a harlot, these shall he not take; but he shall take a virgin of his own people for a wife.

[15] Neither shall he profane his seed among his people, for I the Lord do sanctify him.

[16] And the Lord spoke unto Moses, saying,

[17] Speak unto Aaron, saying, Whosoever he be of thy seed in their generations who hath any blemish, let him not approach to offer the bread of his God.

[18] For whatsoever man he be that hath a blemish, he shall not approach: a blind man, or a lame, or he that hath a flat nose, or any thing superfluous,

[19] or a man who is brokenfooted, or brokenhanded,

[20] or crookbacked, or a dwarf, or who hath a blemish in his eye, or hath scurvy, or scabbed, or hath his stones broken—

[21] no man that hath a blemish of the seed of Aaron the priest shall come nigh to offer the offerings of the Lord made by fire. He hath a blemish: he shall not come nigh to offer the bread of his God.

[22] He shall eat the bread of his God, both of the most holy and of the holy.

[23] Only he shall not go in unto the veil nor come nigh unto the altar, because he hath a blemish, that he profane not My sanctuaries; for I the Lord do sanctify them.

[24] And Moses told it unto Aaron and to his sons, and unto all the children of Israel.

CHAPTER 23

Why You Have Doubts-6

In the book of Numbers the saga continued. Yahweh's behavioral pattern is highlighted once more as He went on a killing rampage, again, roasting humans with fire as depicted in Numbers 11:1, "And when the people complained, it displeased the Lord; and the Lord heard it, and His anger was kindled. And the fire of the Lord burned among them, and consumed those who were in the uttermost parts of the camp."

The description of certain characters of the Bible is interesting. It is so very interesting that if you take a moment to logically match deeds with words, you come up with the worst irrational conclusion any logical mind can come up with. For example, we know that Moses killed his first human in Egypt. You may argue that there was no "Thou shalt not kill" law at the time, therefore, Moses committed no sin. Moses had a free will. He knew that killing a fellow man is atrocious. He knew the gravity of what he did; hence, he ran away from Egypt.

Moses, who now was this murderer, continued to commit murders later, using Yahweh as a cover for his acts. That Moses was described by the Bible as meek in the book of Numbers gave an insight into the workings of the human mind of the writer of Numbers. In other verses, Moses was unashamedly described as the meekest man on the face of the earth.

Numbers 12:3 tells us, (Now the man Moses was very meek, above all the men who were upon the face of the earth.) If Moses was not so meek, he would probably not have been chosen to lead the Israelites.

Below were some of the orders Moses was handed to be executed. Some would argue that he was carrying out an instruction, which, of course, goes further to color the judgments of Moses' Yahweh. Here it is in Numbers 31:13–18:

> [13] And Moses and Eleazar the priest and all the princes of the congregation went forth to meet them outside the camp.

> [14] And Moses was wroth with the officers of the host, with the captains over thousands and captains over hundreds, who came from the battle.

> [15] And Moses said unto them, "Have ye saved all the women alive?

> [16] Behold, these caused the children of Israel, through the counsel of Balaam, to commit trespass against the Lord in the matter of Peor, and there was a plague among the congregation of the Lord.

> [17] Now therefore kill every male among the little ones, and kill every woman who hath known a man by lying with him.

> [18] But all the women children, who have not known a man by lying with him, keep alive for yourselves."

Please pay special attention to verses 17 and 18 above.

Numbers 12:10 informs us, **"And the cloud departed from off the tabernacle**. And behold, Miriam became leprous, white as snow; and Aaron looked upon Miriam, and behold, she was leprous." Take special notice of this verse. It holds the key to most misinterpretations of many verses and chapters of the Bible. To get a very good grasp of the meaning of the word "CLOUD," you must get the book *God Is Not Enough, Messiah*

Needed. In that book, you will learn the meanings of cloud. Once you understand those meanings, as well as understand other words and keep these meanings in mind, try a reread of the Bible and you might, perhaps, get a different perspective.

Numbers 13:33 tells us, "And there we saw the giants, the sons of Anak, who come of the giants. And we were in our own sight as grasshoppers, and so we were in their sight." Were these not the giant children that resulted from the sexual rendezvous of the "sons of God" who could not be kept away from the bosoms of the daughters of men, Genesis 6:4? Are they still on earth? Obviously they are. I have heard and read the many excuses given as explanations for these verses. At the end, it was just some illogical rationalizations where 2 + 2 is never 4. These are not the only areas where the sons of God descriptions were used in the Bible. It was used also in the book of Job 1:6, "Now there was a day when the sons of God came to present themselves before the Lord, and Satan also came among them." It was, and still is, not nice to shift the goal posts during a soccer match. It is an unforgivable behavior that reeks of deceit. Such deceptive intent will incur the wrath of soccer fans.

The Bible was put together as a serious book on a variety of serious subjects that is too often treated as burlesque. The biblical precision language carries the day, irrespective of what revisionists would want us to believe by turning their potential clichés into real feelings and sentiments. Some biblical apologists are too often maudlin, overly cute, and too willing to sacrifice truth to myth. Those seeking excuses for the Bible do so because they don't know any better. It is the same out-churning of indoctrinated ideas which they imbibed from years of gospel according to "Deception."

In Numbers 21:5–8, we read:

> [5] And the people spoke against God and against Moses: "Why have ye brought us up out of Egypt to die in the wilderness? For there is no bread, neither is there any water; and our soul loatheth this light bread."

[6] And the Lord sent fiery serpents among the people, and they bit the people; and many people of Israel died.

[7] Therefore the people came to Moses and said, "We have sinned, for we have spoken against the Lord and against thee. Pray unto the Lord, that He take away the serpents from us." And Moses prayed for the people.

[8] And the Lord said unto Moses, "Make thee a fiery serpent, and set it upon a pole. And it shall come to pass that every one who is bitten, when he looketh upon it, shall live."

Take note that Moses made a graven image so that whoever took a look at it would live. That was fine saving the people, but remember in Exodus 20:4, "Thou shalt not make unto thee any graven image, or any likeness of anything that is in heaven above, or that is in the earth beneath, or that is in the water under the earth." You can draw your own conclusions here.

CHAPTER 24

Why You Have Doubts-7

Yahweh was a God of war. He was a God that engages in wars. War is defined as a conflict, combat, warfare, fighting, confrontation, hostilities, battles, etc. By all accounts, war is the destruction of an enemy. If Yahweh was the creator of all mankind, why was He so in love in edifying His actions as a warrior, destroying the same humans He created? It was like He hated these other peoples so much as if they were created by those other gods whom Yahweh has instructed His new children not to worship. That Yahweh was a warmonger is no longer in doubt because He makes a PowerPoint of that in His résumé, like in Deuteronomy 3:22, "Ye shall not fear them, for the Lord your God He shall fight for you."

Reading through the book *Why Was Man Created?* we find no place or description where the creator of man was engaged in man's destruction. Every single challenge man has faced, the creator was lurking around through all manner of logistical plans to save His creation like a parent would do to save his children. On the other hand, Yahweh was always portrayed (even as edifying) as a monstrous murderer who gets his highs at the amount of blood—human or animals. Read the Bible. No one is making this up.

Often, a narrative is found that was descriptive of Yahweh's modus operandi, and after careful analysis, some resort to descriptive terms that are not so palatable to the ears and you wonder why. For example, how would you look at a side in a war that goes on to annihilate its opponents (combatants and noncombatants alike), children, and women (Deuteronomy 7:2, 16), and . . . later is advised to love their enemies? (Deuteronomy 10:19)

As if in confirmation of the above, chapter 7:14–16 suggests measures at reduction of other peoples; thus:

[14] Thou shalt be blessed above all people. There shall not be male or female barren among you or among your cattle.

[15] And the Lord will take away from thee all sickness, and will put none of the evil diseases of Egypt, which thou knowest, upon thee, but will lay them upon all those who hate thee.

[16] And thou shalt consume all the people which the Lord thy God shall deliver thee; thine eye shall have no pity upon them; neither shalt thou serve their gods, for that will be a snare unto thee.

So that all future generation might see and read all about this Yahweh, He instructs mankind, in chapter 4:2, "You shall not add to the word which I command you, nor take from it, that you may keep the commandments of the LORD your God which I command you."

And there is a warning to bastards and those whose testicles are neutered from chapter 23:

[1] "He that is wounded in the stones or hath his private member cut off shall not enter into the congregation of the Lord.

[2] A bastard shall not enter into the congregation of the Lord; even to his tenth generation shall he not enter into the congregation of the Lord.

And how to defecate was important to God because He would hate to step on excreta while walking around the community's living quarters. Chapter 23:12–14 explains:

¹² "Thou shalt have a place also outside the camp whither thou shalt go forth abroad.

¹³ And thou shalt have a paddle upon thy weapon; and it shall be, when thou wilt ease thyself abroad, thou shalt dig therewith, and shalt turn back and cover that which cometh from thee.

¹⁴ For the Lord thy God walketh in the midst of thy camp to deliver thee and to give up thine enemies before thee; therefore shall thy camp be holy, that He see no unclean thing in thee and turn away from thee."

The miracle of Deuteronomy—one of the five books written by Moses—was exposed in chapter 34:4–6.

That Moses recorded his death and how he was buried was/is miraculous. I only wished he narrated the spot where he was buried. What a man! What a prophet! If not for chapter 12:32, the canonizers of the Bible may have yanked this miracle.

In the book of Numbers 6, 9, and 19, we were cautioned about corpses. We read that it would make those who come in contact with a corpse become unclean. Chapter 19:11–15 made this very clear when you read, "'He that toucheth the dead body of any man shall be unclean seven days.

¹² He shall purify himself with the water on the third day, and on the seventh day he shall be clean; but if he purify not himself the third day, then the seventh day he shall not be clean.

¹³ Whosoever toucheth the dead body of any man who is dead and purifieth not himself, defileth the tabernacle of the Lord, and that soul shall be cut off from Israel. Because the water of separation was not sprinkled upon him, he shall be unclean; his uncleanness is yet upon him.

[14] ""This is the law when a man dieth in a tent: All who come into the tent, and all who are in the tent, shall be unclean seven days.

[15] And every open vessel, which hath no covering bound upon it, is unclean.

ALSO . . .
In Leviticus 21:11, neither shall he go in to any dead body, nor defile himself for his father or for his mother;

WHEREAS . . .
In Deuteronomy 34:5–6, we read:

[5] "So Moses the servant of the Lord died there in the land of Moab, according to the word of the Lord.

[6] And He buried him in a valley in the land of Moab, over against Bethpeor; but no man knoweth of his sepulcher unto this day.

Here, Yahweh buried Moses. Whether He touched Moses' corpse is not known. Whether He magically commanded the corpse into the pit is left to imagination. However, when it is written of burial of corpses, our minds know what it means. If God buried Moses through some miraculous way, it would have been so written. This point is made particularly to underline disparities in statutes. At a given time, a statute is right; and at another time, that same statute would be considered a sin.

Do you ever wonder why priests today perform burial rites? Obviously, they have stubbornly refused to follow Yahweh's commands. It is either that or they have chosen to misinterpret the books or maybe the books have contradicting texts. Whichever one it is, is it in anyone's place to challenge the narrations?

One more flagrant contradiction: Leviticus 17:15–16, Deuteronomy 14:21.

Deuteronomy 14:21 states: "Ye shall not eat of any thing that dieth of itself. Thou shalt give it unto the stranger who is in thy gates, that he may eat it, or thou mayest sell it unto an alien; for thou art a holy people unto the Lord thy God. "Thou shalt not boil a kid in his mother's milk."

Leviticus 17:15: And every soul that eateth that which died of itself or that which was torn by beasts, whether it be one of your own country or a stranger, he shall both wash his clothes and bathe himself in water, and be unclean until the evening; then shall he be clean.

> [16] But if he wash them not nor bathe his flesh, then he shall bear his iniquity.'"

Do you read the contradiction there? It was, and still probably is, that Yahweh does not view mankind as the same. Have you ever asked yourself why this was/is so? Clue: Maybe if He created mankind, He would not segregate as such. At this juncture, if you have yet to read the books *Why Was Man Created?* and *God Is Not Enough, Messiah Needed,* you are not doing yourself any favors.

As you ponder on the chapters of confusion and contrasts, think about this. In 2 Kings 2:23–25, Elisha the prophet was jeered: Below was how he dealt with his dilemma.

> [23] And he went up from thence unto Bethel: and as he was going up by the way, there came forth little children out of the city, and mocked him, and said unto him, Go up, thou bald head; go up, thou bald head.

> [24] And he turned back, and looked on them, and cursed them in the name of the Lord. And there came forth two she bears out of the wood, and tare forty and two children of them.

> [25] And he went from thence to mount Carmel, and from thence he returned to Samaria.

Came out of the city and mocked him . . . Go up, you bald head. Mockery denotes a scornful belittling of something or someone, but it issues from an attitude which counts as valueless that which is really of great value. But, even at that, how can one who serves his Lord do this to little children?

Today, our leaders have always had to deal with disrespect. The event described in these verses is very repulsive to many and totally out of character with the personality of a man of God. This is nothing but deadly use of vengeance upon a group of playful, naughty kids carried out in the name of his Lord. Not surprisingly, Elisha chose to demonstrate some characteristics he learned. Perhaps he learned such dispensation of justice from the Lord. That is, the use of wanton deadly force. How characteristic of such legal dispensation conniving with the Lord.

Now that you have read all the chapters titled "Why You Have Doubts," let us do some homework, and it is also from the book of 2 Kings 2 (KJV). Let us now read and interpret some verses from 2 Kings 2 (KJV). Pay special attention to verse 11. Do you remember the interpretation given for Ezekiel 10? If yes, what do you think of "chariots of fire" and "horses of fire"? Do you understand what/which heaven Elijah was taken to when it was written, "Elijah went up by a whirlwind into heaven"? If you have a problem figuring this out, I will advise you to do a recap of the book *God Is Not Enough, Messiah Needed.*

2 Kings 2:1–12:

2 And it came to pass, when the Lord would take up Elijah into heaven by a whirlwind, that Elijah went with Elisha from Gilgal.

² And Elijah said unto Elisha, Tarry here, I pray thee; for the Lord hath sent me to Bethel. And Elisha said unto him, As the Lord liveth, and as thy soul liveth, I will not leave thee. So they went down to Bethel.

³ And the sons of the prophets that were at Bethel came forth to Elisha, and said unto him, Knowest thou that the Lord will take away thy master from thy head to day? And he said, Yea, I know it; hold ye your peace.

⁴ And Elijah said unto him, Elisha, tarry here, I pray thee; for the Lord hath sent me to Jericho. And he said, As the Lord liveth, and as thy soul liveth, I will not leave thee. So they came to Jericho.

⁵ And the sons of the prophets that were at Jericho came to Elisha, and said unto him, Knowest thou that the Lord will take away thy master from thy head to day? And he answered, Yea, I know it; hold ye your peace.

⁶ And Elijah said unto him, Tarry, I pray thee, here; for the Lord hath sent me to Jordan. And he said, As the Lord liveth, and as thy soul liveth, I will not leave thee. And they two went on.

⁷ And fifty men of the sons of the prophets went, and stood to view afar off: and they two stood by Jordan.

⁸ And Elijah took his mantle, and wrapped it together, and smote the waters, and they were divided hither and thither, so that they two went over on dry ground.

⁹ And it came to pass, when they were gone over, that Elijah said unto Elisha, Ask what I shall do for thee, before I be taken away from thee. And Elisha said, I pray thee, let a double portion of thy spirit be upon me.

¹⁰ And he said, Thou hast asked a hard thing: nevertheless, if thou see me when I am taken from thee, it shall be so unto thee; but if not, it shall not be so.

[11] And it came to pass, as they still went on, and talked, that, behold, there appeared a chariot of fire, and horses of fire, and parted them both asunder; and Elijah went up by a whirlwind into heaven.

[12] And Elisha saw it, and he cried, My father, my father, the chariot of Israel, and the horsemen thereof. And he saw him no more: and he took hold of his own clothes, and rent them in two pieces.

CHAPTER 25

Conclusion

Photo: Courtesy iStockphoto

The point of research is not to make connections or dots to fit your already established view on a particular topic. You let the research lead to the facts, no matter how much you hate that fact. And you state the fact as is. When you engage in an argument with facts you will make a good argument, and not just for the entertainment value—it can be a good learning experience. Personally, I value intellectual honesty a great deal. And that intellectual honesty could be a simple problem of $2 + 2 = 4$.

One of the reasons for this work is to help channel some of the multitude of Bible readers and readers of books of other religious doctrines in the direction of logic and reason. The truth is that most Jews, Christians, and, indeed, others, who read the Bible and other books like it, have no idea how and what to believe, so they believe by faith. These ancient texts were produced by royal scribes and religious leaders in powerful economic and political positions and settings. They wrote to advocate and make legitimate particular political or religious ideas and reforms to yield desired doctrines and ideologies. Like we saw in the interpretation of chapter 10 of the book of Ezekiel, even the best versed people in Bible narratives hardly understand the book. This writer is a strong believer in free will with the understanding that man will always find a balance to succeed in whatever man sets his mind to accomplish. If left alone, an average man can read the Bible and interpret it for himself because man can make a decision for self. But that simple task may have been taken away and replaced by a forced "free will" of faith. *Faith!* That word! Faith is *not* free will because free will must not be controlled, because any control renders free will no longer free. Free will manipulated is not free will. Apart from rules, covenants, and commandments which make free will redundant, FAITH is a commandment camouflaged to mean strong belief in an untested dogma. Faith is fear, and thus, it is the systematic marketing of fear. Freedom of thought otherwise called the freedom of conscience or ideas is the freedom of an individual to hold a viewpoint, or thought, totally independent of societal viewpoints.

"Freedom of thought" is the derivative of and most often closely linked to other liberties, such as these freedoms.

1. Freedom of religion,

2. Freedom of speech, and

3. Freedom of expression.

    When these freedoms are compromised the result is anarchy. The attempt to limit the freedoms listed above curtails our enjoyment of other freedoms, including the right to life. When societies refuse to allow you to think freely about ideas and beliefs, it trickles down to all human rights. The result of such happenings are all over the place for everyone to see, and indeed, the oppression of thought by the state is a sign of weakness and insecurity, rather than that of strength. Freedom of thought to enable your belief and religion is a good thing.

In most societies people have rights to freedom of thought, belief, and religion. In some societies, people are still fighting for these rights. In others, these rights are written into the constitutions and are open to interpretations if disagreements arise.

When we enjoy these freedoms, we are participating in the process of applying logic or reason, science, and empiricism to questions of belief and eschewing reliance on dogma, tradition, and authority. It's important to note that this definition is about the methodology and tools one uses to arrive at beliefs, not the actual beliefs a person ends up with. This means freethinking is at least theoretically compatible with a wide range of actual beliefs.

You also have the right to put your thoughts and beliefs into action. For example, public authorities cannot stop you practicing your religion, publicly or privately, without very good reason, as outlined in the restrictions.

Importantly, this right protects a wide range of religious beliefs and other beliefs, including veganism, pacifism, agnosticism, and atheism. When a work is written, it could be a work or an idea expressed that is very unpopular, yet they are expressed without fear of persecution for the expressed thought. Thus, freedom of thought is a right to hold unpopular ideas.

There was, and probably still is, a time in man's history where the refrain was—*I am a Christian. They can ridicule and disparage me. They can torture and imprison me. They can even kill me for my thoughts; however, you cannot change my mind for I believe by faith.* Now, there is a new refrain. *I am an atheist. Once, some Christians ridiculed and disparaged certain thoughts. They tortured and even killed many of us for a very long time in hopes of coercing me to their side. They made efforts to force me to accept their teachings. I held steadfast to my thoughts knowing full well that no ideas worth believing require extreme coercion. I want to be able to change my mind if reasonable evidence is presented to warrant a change of belief.* I want to have an open mind. For many whose only mode of thought is "faith," it will be easier for them to swim up Niagara Falls than accept logical thought processes. People should be free even if free means to jump from the frying pan into the fire. After all, this is free thought—opinions about questions of religion formed independently of tradition, authority, or established belief. Many people attach much more importance to the "why" of belief than to the "what." Such people believe in the sort of human understanding that naturally follows from a careful and rational consideration of the relevant factual evidence—not faith. However, I believe strongly that careful and rational consideration of relevant factual evidence can also reinforce faith.

I regard the scientific method as the proper approach and scientific knowledge as the most reliable sort of human understanding. And yes, there is an abundance of science narratives in the Bible too. If you read my book *Why Was Man Created?* you would have observed that many of the chapters reflect science concepts.

Most of us want to believe that life must have a purpose. Some believe that if life is to have authentic meaning, we must create it or discover it for ourselves. After reading and answering the question *Why Was Man Created?* would it not be considered foolish to live life in compliance with or in obedience to someone else's purpose, even the unknowable purpose(s) of those who reengineered us? To do so is to live according to the reason we were reengineered.

This work, like others written by this author, has not sought in any way or fashion to debunk the existence of superintelligent beings mankind has come to call God. If anything, historical biblical records give us insight to their existence.

Most of the people that are close to me view the nature of reality differently than I do. Sometimes, for the sake of not getting into an unnecessary tug-of-war on beliefs, I do what they are doing belief-wise just to fit in. But I'm tired of doing that. They believe in a divine creator, a soul destined for an afterlife, and a Bible containing God's words. I have spent no small amount of time during the last 6 years of my life reviewing the evidence for these claims, and have found the evidence that:

1. That there was a visitation of intelligent beings

2. That the universe was already in existence before the visitation to planet Earth

3. That modern-day man was a result of reengineering, and finally

4. These intelligent beings are not from the beginning of time (Universal Creator).

While you ponder on these thoughts, here is another reason for this book.

Let us use logic and reason: Reading the Bible and finding its interpretation, especially for apocalyptic readings, is neither found in a crystal ball nor a horror show. It would even be smarter to etch-a-sketch the Bible, for this would allow dialogue of "If we are wrong, we wipe off the slate and start afresh." Thus, we can deal better with topics such as dispensationalism—a coinage for rapture theology. Rapture theology has led to bad theology because of bad biblical interpretations. It has led to doctrines and ideas that are foreign to the texts of scriptures because of bad interpretations. Because of rapture theology, many followers have had a mind-set of "the end is near" syndrome right from the "ascension" of Jesus Christ. The "end is near" syndrome in itself is a confusing doctrine like many other doctrines. Some of us have had the fortune— nay misfortune—of witnessing leaders lead their parishioners to death because they invented interpretations that were neither here nor there. The rapture is a bogus doctrine with no legitimate basis in scripture. By use of the rapture theology, dispensationalists claim that the "end is near" which was and still is in direct contradiction of the Gospels where Jesus was credited as teaching that no one but God knows the time of the end (Mark 13:32). Hmm! I just smiled at that quote for even Jesus Himself does not know. But He should have, based on the dogma of the Triune. It should be said here and now that although Paul did seem to believe that the end was near, by the time that the Gospels were written, that sensibility seems to have evaporated and condensed into a more patient expectation of the future. This rapture theology interpretation may have caused and may still be causing some havoc today. Two examples come to mind:

1. Plant crazy ideas in people's minds as in scare tactics to undermine attempts to save the planet. Why save the planet if, according to rapture theology, the end is near?

2. Becomes an enabling threshold for illogical and dangerous support for those who would undermine efforts to bring peace in the Middle East so that the "will of the Lord" would prevail.

Though we know that the biblical text is a book revered by people of faith, if it is to be understood, it must be interpreted with common sense and logic and not under the influence of "possession" by "the spirit of the LORD." The Bible was written for man—ordinary men like you and me. It was not written for prophets who speak under the influence of "tongues" and "divine direction." Interpretation must be done carefully and skillfully, applying common sense, not implying "influence of anything." If the reader of the scripture is to be best served, there should be no introduction of things and meanings that are not implied in a text. Some interpreters tend to have a mind-set that they could go to Kentucky Fried Chicken and get a nice meal of fried veggies. Some people can always interpret the Bible for all their "wrong reasons," but not for our "all the right reasons." They tend to do this over and over again, not knowing they are brewing a beer named trouble. Therefore, it is important when reading and interpreting the Bible to consider the nature and settings of a particular biblical text and to ask questions appropriate to that text within that setting. That faith slogan of He is the same yesterday, today, and will be the same tomorrow, should be applied logically too, for it has been demonstrated that immutability teaching is man's invention.

We must accept that to understand the Bible you must come with an unadulterated mind. Biblical criticism is nothing but the scholarly study and investigation of biblical writings that seeks to make discerning logical and reasonable judgments about its narratives. You are allowed and encouraged to view biblical texts as having human, rather than supernatural, origins. You must ask where and when a particular text originated; it's setting, how, why, by whom, for whom, and in what circumstances a narrative was produced; what influences were at work in its production; what sources were used in its composition; and what message it was intended to convey.

Another reason for this book is this: that revelation has been frequently defined in opposition to reason because reason is the natural exercise of human mental capacities in search of knowledge while revelation is when we bypass these faculties and gain knowledge by way of education. A case can be made that this distinction between reason and revelation is already present. There was a time in human existence—a time when human wisdom and insight were everywhere understood to be the gift of the gods.

Another good reason for this work is a passion to uproot idiocy and/or hypocrisy. When one chooses one of the established religions, you have narrowed your options to two: an idiot, or the alternative, a hypocrite. And that is what most religious people practice—hypocrisy. They stand there acting like they are better than everyone else. They pretend that they are practicing and living the divine laws in the daylight for all to see. They are very worried of the judgments of their peers. It is like a battle for who is more pious than piety itself. They act like they are the oasis of morality in a desert full of sinners, as if their dogma is standard for world morals. To these groups of fanatics, rationalizing has replaced rational. To them, education, science evidence, and reason can no longer help and advance man. By rationalizing all the illogical and pervasive doctrines they practice, they are quick to use deadly force, even if thousands of deaths are recorded. In their zealotry, stupidity has risen to the threshold of religious dogma; they are closed minded to rational thinking. If a logical thinking person associates with these dogma-worshipping practitioners, if they did not need a shrink initially—they would certainly need one as soon as disengagement occurs.

Here is a riddle: A father and a son went out for a car ride. During the ride, the car crashed and the father died, but the son sustained injuries. The son was rushed to a specialist hospital for emergency surgery. But, when the surgeon took one look at the boy, the surgeon said, "I cannot operate on this patient because he is my son." Please STOP and make a guess on the relationship of the surgeon to the son before reading further. Did you guess right? How long did it take you to come up with the answer to the riddle?

If you were a fan of the TV series *All In The Family,* you may quickly come up with the answer really fast. That many people could not come up with the answer today is because many folks still have the mind-set of yesteryears. I know because I asked numerous people on the streets. I spoke to a random population of 100 people. Out of them, 40 (men and women) of at least 50 or more years were part of the population. The remaining 60 were a combination of ages, mostly 49 and below. These included an approximate 40 percent of religion-practicing individuals. It was a surprise that only about 5 percent got the answer to the riddle. It was not a surprise that very few had the answer to the riddle. This is because our smartness is shaped by our perception of the environment we grew up in. Our perception of the environment of the medical profession, with specificity to surgeons, is that it is comprised of men. The difficulty in figuring out the answer to the riddle was due to our perception confusion, not the difficulty of the riddle. By the way, the answer to the riddle is the boy's mother.

Most interpretations of the holy books are the casualty of perception. Cultures worldwide have heavily impacted our outlook on life and, thus, behaviors. Any wonder a harmless kiss in public in the United States is viewed as bad behavior in Northern Nigeria? Or the clobbering of an animal in public in one place viewed as inhumane in other places?

The various religions on the planet acknowledge and attest by their actions voluntarily or otherwise, the contradictions, contrasts, misinterpretations, and disagreements about God's words or statutes in the many stories of the good book. Do your own study and write down all the observable differences you can notice among readers of the books of the Bible and you may wonder why it is so. Among the biblical followers are various sects—Catholic and Protestants. Among the Protestants you have more protesting. Protestants!—That word! I love that word, for in this matter, you may ask—What are they protesting? They are protesting the confusion and "misrepresentation" and misinterpretation of the words of the Bible. Some are even protesting Protestants. Some are so quick to say that there is no confusion, no contrasts, no misinterpretation, yet they are living the confusion day in and day out.

Some are quick to defend the book, quoting unrelated verses from the body of chapters to prove why God does not create confusion, whereas God Himself was in black and white as saying, let us go down and create confusion for man using language. The only concluding logic one can draw from any verse or verses to contradict what God said in the book of Genesis about creating confusion for man is in themselves contradictory. Therefore, they confirm unwittingly the line of argument that there was, and still is, contradictions, contrasts, and misrepresentations in the Bible.

The Bible in its crudest form is more straightforward and honest than all the apologists, fanatics, and clergy that claim to live by its teachings. The Bible in all its honest narratives presented a God who is crude and wicked, a being lacking in tolerance, a warmonger, magician, and a protector, and a God who sometimes is indecisive, just like man whom He allegedly claimed to have created. The Bible is so honest that sometimes it forgets it has an agenda—the agenda of those who chose what books belonged in the Bible. To that extent, the Bible describes an event, rather than expresses an opinion. It is therefore an event left to your interpretation; hence, the many misinterpretations given to literal words by some clergy which are just that—literal.

Most often, you see the manipulation of the hand of man in the interpretations of the Bible, but try as they could, the truth of each chapter still shines through for those who have no set agenda. The Bible is simply a bank for knowledge to understanding beings who had been here eons of years before they decided to reengineer mankind to take their place on earth. If you understand this, you will ultimately come to the conclusion that all the maiming, killing, alienation, suffering, and all the wars that were fought just to promote monotheism and monotheistic teachings seem to have been a waste of effort and in itself a war fought by confused minds. A war mandated by people whose minds were controlled by lunacy and confusion. For even after those wars were fought in the name of religion, the only legacy it left is not one of clear-cut monotheism. If there is anything clear-cut of a legacy, it is that of confusion. It is a legacy of confused monotheism. And as if all that isn't confusing enough, today, more than ever before, we have these supposedly definitive monotheist religions full of splinter groups, sects, factions, cliques, schisms, and in-fighting. When it comes to the attributes of God and the best way of worshipping Him, none of these sects and factions can agree on anything—and you can count yourself lucky if the discussion of religious matters does not terminate in explosions.

There are so many different views of the One true God; it sometimes seems that all those schisms, factions, and sects are really desperately yearning for the good old days of polytheism, which is probably the ultimate irony.

The best cure for ignorance in any sphere of human endeavor is education. The best cure for the confusions and doubts in the Bible is to read the Bible over and over again. Thus, the best cure for a confused religionist is to study your type of holy book. I have read a couple of religious books and found out that the biggest problems are not the narratives in themselves but *interpreters* of the narratives. This is because even when the truth can be found there within, misinterpretations by others have led many astray. The best cure to believing by faith, and faith alone, is to read the book. The best support to ground your beliefs is evidence . . . lots of it. And the best way to build that framework structure of support is to read and connect dots from your past and present education, some of which are found in the holy books, science, archaeology, history, etc. Do not take anyone's side. Read and establish your own side for yourself. Do not discard science while reading the Bible. Do not also think that you are so good in science, therefore, there is nothing to gain from the Bible. Our problem as man is that we think we are the first smart living things in the universe, even when we all know now that the earth is much younger than the universe.

Finally, let us attempt to limit confusion anywhere that it may exist. Some of the principles for interpreting narratives can be found in my previous book *God Is Not Enough, Messiah Needed,* but below are more principles specifically related to understanding the narratives.

Read through the entire biblical narrative to understand the plot, flow, purpose, and major themes of that narrative. Imagine the setting, and then read narrative as is, being careful not to introduce or conjure what was not in the narrative. Most of us have grown up with the Gospels or Old Testament history as isolated stories. Therefore, the first step is to sit down and read the entire narrative from beginning to end. Most of us seldom sit down to simply read through the narratives to catch the drama and power of the stories as they fit together to form a holistic panorama. We must, therefore, absorb within us that the first step is to sit down and read the entire narrative from beginning to end. Anything less is disingenuous to self.

Ask yourself what you think the author tried to establish—The authors had a reason and purpose for writing. What are these purposes? Remember that the biblical narratives were written by authors who had a purpose in writing a narrative. Do not inject any spirituality to interpret the parts of narratives apart from the big picture purpose of the authors. If the writers wanted spirituality, they would have injected it themselves. I cannot hammer home this point more than I did with the book of Prophet Ezekiel.

Every author has a message, information they want to get across to the reader, and this is true of writers of biblical narratives. An example is John. John explains that the reason he wrote his Gospel was so that his readers might know and believe that Jesus is the Christ, the Son of God (see John 20:31). Again, without infusing spirituality, being the Son of God is simply what it means. The narration of the conception of Jesus simply attests to the literal meaning.

This point of view guides the reader to the significance of the story and determines the actual modification that the author gives to the narrative. You, the reader, must establish a good understanding of the historical and cultural contexts of the narratives. Also, for you to truly understand what is taking place in a biblical narrative you must be familiar with the surroundings in which the narrative took place. Not to understand this is the reason why many interpreters invent unseen and unexciting, fearful spirits.

Once you can foundationally establish that narratives are not just stories about Bible characters but stories told of God and how God worked through the characters, plots, and events, and bearing in mind that God is the hero of all biblical narratives, you will find it difficult to infuse your biases. You start seeing the logic, the illogicalities, and reasons for a given narrative. By now, you would have noticed that narratives often do not teach doctrine directly.

Have it at the back of your mind that a narrative recorded what actually happened, not what *should* have happened. To draw morals from such happenings seem like drawing a moral from historical events. The point is not every narrative has an individual identifiable moral of the story because narratives do not answer all of our theological questions. This does not mean, though, that one cannot learn doctrine from biblical narratives. There is this fear—a worrisome one too—that interpreters will start seeking hidden meanings in narratives. There are no hidden meanings at all in the narratives. If the authors intended to hide things from us they would not have written the books for all to read.

THE BOOK OF GENESIS AND TIME:

The issue of creationism is ultimately not one of just facts as we learn daily through the sciences. Such empirical evidence could be an avenue for reinforcement of faith. This should be the mind-set you should have while reading the book of Genesis. You should endeavor to interpret the book literally, in the light of the culture and customs of its day. However, to read the book literally without applying common empirical evidence provided by the sciences create some serious problems in understanding. The first chapter of the Bible says that God made heaven and earth and every living thing in 6 days. Are those 6 "days" to be understood literally, as 6 24-hour days?

You know that the universe is approximately 14.7 billion years old. We also now know that the Earth is approximately 4.6 billion years old. By faith, Bible-believing Christians will disagree on this. They sometimes condemn all who do not understand Genesis 1 in the same way as they do. But you have the facts, and thus, you stand on good grounds. You have evidence. Make up your mind based on facts and your belief will be grounded by facts.

Do not start reading the Bible in confusion. Have this perspective when you are dealing with Genesis of the Bible. Divide the Bible into two. First part is Genesis Chapter One and perhaps Chapter Two, and the second part is the rest of the Bible. The first part happened billions of years ago. The second part happened later with the reengineering of man.

Some theologians would want you to believe that Genesis 1–11 covers thousands of years, while Genesis 12–50 covers just a few hundred years. I do not buy into that argument. By now, you too may be having doubts on that declaration. You should . . . because it is not reasonable. With this mind-set, you will start to see things in perspective. Meanwhile, the explanation of what constitutes a day is contained in the book *Why Was Man Created?* See pages 5–6.

God and the scientists: Are science and faith at war? Does science undermine or corroborate belief in God? If you listen to some you may think that they are at war. Some have suggested that science undermines religion, while others say religion is a tool for control. There are those who will claim that faith suppresses scientific research. Some even suggest that the sphere of supernatural influence will eventually shrink to almost zero. These and other questions should be areas religion must seek to answer the questions raised. If I am to believe in a Universal Creator, I want to be a smart believer who can explain scientific findings. Over time, it appears that science is slowly but gradually chipping away at the traditional reasons for believing in God. And that reason for belief is hugely founded on faith. Science, by its very nature, seems to help reinterpret narratives of the Bible. Much of what once seemed spiritual—the essence of biblical God and the workings of the universe—can now be easily explained by biology, astronomy, quantum physics, mathematics, etc. It is as if God's sphere of influence has shrunk drastically in modern times, as physics and cosmology have taken over following their ability to explain the origin and evolution of the universe. But could science really eventually explain everything? The thing is this:

When science says the earth is round, it harmonizes with Isaiah 40:22.

When science says man has Y-chromosomes and women X-chromosomes seeds of life, it harmonizes with Genesis 3:15.

When science say they discovered gravity, the Bible narrated that before science in Job 26:7.

There are persons who argue that God's sphere of influence has shrunk drastically in modern times as the sciences and cosmology have expanded in their ability to explain the origin and evolution of the universe. But while science is discovering and harmonizing the Bible narratives, such narratives were already existent before science explained some. Over the course of time I have read voraciously many a book on sciences, and especially quantum physics. I also know that the debate between scientists and religious believers is as contentious as ever, but should there be contention? Of course, there will be when some people faithfully believe that the earth is 6,000 years old.

The point is, science knowledge can be very instrumental to solidifying one's faith, for indeed, as you have seen in this book, parts of the Bible are interpreted wrongly.

Before Einstein—perhaps the greatest scientist ever—before Newton's discoveries, before Galileo, there were narratives of technology, biology, and astronomy in the Bible. It just took man a little too long to catch up with the actual interpretation. Perhaps we are still reinterpreting.

The major criticisms of religion made in the past few hundred years under the umbrella of modern science should not be waved off as noise from the unbelievers; instead, it should be taken with the utmost seriousness. It could be an avenue to learn from reasonable arguments of contemporary atheism, for as we have seen in this book, reasonable arguments could be resources for building a stronger faith where the foundation is anchored in facts.

I hope you found this an interesting and thought-provoking book, especially for lay readers of scripture. If read with the cap of logic and common sense, the book offers wisdom, insight, and principles of interpretation that would channel you along the lines of defined belief, not based on faith but on facts. Perhaps after reading this book, you will be able to more wisely read the Bible for all the right reasons and right interpretations, thereby yanking out all the wrong assumptions, wrong imageries, and borrowed interpretations from your mind.

Bibliography

BIBLE QUOTES FROM

http://www.biblegateway.com/versions/King-James-Version-KJV-Bible

New International Version (NIV)

New King James Version. 1982. Thomas Nelson Inc.

King James Version. 1611. www.kingjamesbibleonline.org/1611-Bible/

Oputa, Sam. 2014. *Why Was Man Created? War Of the Gods*. Outskirts Press. Denver, Colorado.

Oputa, Sam. 2013. *God Is Not Enough, Messiah Needed*. Outskirts Press. Denver, Colorado.

OTHER ONLINE RESOURCES:

Austine Cline from about.com Web site (Ref: http://atheism.about.com/od/Bible-Study-Pentateuch/a/Book-Exodus-Intro.htm).

"Doubting the Story of Exodus" (Ref: http://www.aish.com/ci/sam/48938472.html).

Coffman, James Burton. "Commentary on Ezekiel 10:1." *Coffman Commentaries on the Old and New Testament.* http://www.studylight. org/com/bcc/view.cgi?book=eze&chapter=010. Abilene Christian University Press, Abilene, Texas, USA. 1983–1999.

Ezekiel's Chapter 10 Interpretation, online resource: (Ref: http://www.finaltrump.com/2009/06/ezekiel-chapter-10/)

Kenneth Cauthen: Church and State, Politics and Religion http://www.frontiernet.net/~kenc/relandpo.htm

Shmoop.com (http://www.shmoop.com/genesis/summary.html

Wiki.answers (Ref: http://wiki.answers.com/Q/ What_evidence_is_there_that_the_Bible_is_divinely_inspired)

DIAGRAMS AND ILLUSTRATIONS:

All in the Family, the CBS TV series

How Merciful Is God? Credit for the above table: http://skepticsannotatedbible.com/contra/merciful.html

www.ingramcontent.com/pod-product-compliance
Lightning Source LLC
Chambersburg PA
CBHW071149050326
40689CB00011B/2041